Innovator's
Toolkit

Harvard Business Essentials

The New Manager's Guide and Mentor

The Harvard Business Essentials series is designed to provide comprehensive advice, personal coaching, background information, and guidance on the most relevant topics in business. Drawing on rich content from Harvard Business School Publishing and other sources, these concise guides are carefully crafted to provide a highly practical resource for readers with all levels of experience, and will prove especially valuable for the new manager. To assure quality and accuracy, each volume is closely reviewed by a specialized content adviser from a world-class business school. Whether you are a new manager seeking to expand your skills or a seasoned professional looking to broaden your knowledge base, these solution-oriented books put reliable answers at your fingertips.

Other books in the series:

Finance for Managers
Hiring and Keeping the Best People
Managing Change and Transition
Negotiation
Business Communication
Managing Projects Large and Small
Manager's Toolkit
Crisis Management
Entrepreneur's Toolkit
Time Management
Power, Influence, and Persuasion
Strategy
Decision Making
Marketer's Toolkit
Performance Management
Coaching and Mentoring
Managing Teams with an Edge
Managing Creativity and Innovation

Innovator's Toolkit

*10 Practical Strategies to Help You
Develop and Implement Innovation*

Harvard Business Press | *Boston, Massachusetts*

ISBN 13: 978-1-4221-9990-9

The paper used in this publication meets the requirements of the American
National Standard for Permanence of Paper for Publications
and Documents in Libraries and Archives Z39.48-1992.

Contents

Innovator's
Toolkit

Introduction

Innovation has shaped human society and daily life in every age. Its power is such that historians and archeologists today define broad periods of human history in terms of the innovations that have distinguished them: the Stone Age, the Bronze Age, the Iron Age, the Industrial Age, the Atomic Age, the Digital Age, and so forth. While each of these labels refers to a technology, innovation is much broader than technology. Indeed, the impact of innovation can be seen over the centuries in such diverse areas of human endeavor as religion, social organization, architecture, military tactics, medicine, agriculture, and the arts.

Even periods popularly regarded as stagnant have been altered importantly by technological innovation. For example, the heavy moldboard plow, the three-field system of crop rotation, the stirrup, and vertical- and horizontal-axle windmills were all either invented or adopted in northern Europe during the early Middle Ages, and each created substantial change in people's lives. Let's consider two of these.

Historians believe that the heavy moldboard plow originated among the Slavs and was introduced by seventh-century Goths to northern Europe, where the soil was almost impenetrable to the "scratch plow," the prevailing technology of the day. The scratch plow had been used in southern climes since Roman days. Its key feature was a vertical, triangular "share" (iron or wood) which, dragged behind a pair of oxen, was adequate for cutting a narrow furrow in the dry, thin soils of the Mediterranean region. But for the heavy, damp earth of northern Europe, something more robust was required. The moldboard plow had three basic elements: a coulter, or heavy vertical knife, that cut into the soil; a plowshare set at right angles to the coulter for horizontal cutting; and a moldboard designed to turn the heavy earth to one side. This new device greatly increased agricultural productivity in transalpine Europe and allowed farmers to cultivate fertile alluvial areas that until that time had been unworkable.

The stirrup was another innovation that altered society in medieval Europe. According to the late historian Lynn White Jr., the eighth-century introduction of the iron stirrup from India gave the mounted warrior battlefield ascendancy. Using stirrups for support, he could deliver a blow, not with the strength of his own arm, but with the vastly greater power of his horse.[1] This greater capacity altered the role of the mounted warrior, who since ancient times had been limited to scouting and flanking. The armored man on horseback was now the master of the battlefield, and that mastery quickly spilled over into social and political power. The medieval knight would remain at the pinnacle of society and warfare until the fifteenth and sixteenth centuries, when new innovations—the tactical use of the Welsh longbow, and then firearms—changed the game.

Though the term *innovation* entered the English vocabulary in the fifteenth century, it's probably safe to say that few people prior to the nineteenth century used it regularly. Not so today. The term is now used routinely and is the subject of university courses, scholarly studies, books, and articles. Recognizing that innovation is the catalyst of economic progress and national competitiveness, government and business leaders demand innovation and periodically launch programs to encourage more of it.

The Role of Innovation in Enterprise

Innovation that the marketplace values has long been recognized as a creator and sustainer of enterprise. Every time Intel's engineers produce a new generation of computer chips that customers value, its fortunes are renewed. Whenever a pharmaceutical company introduces a drug that restores the health of millions around the globe, it too gains a new lease on life. When a PC service firm thinks of a way to fix a customer's computer software over the Internet, that company opens up a new channel for growth.

Innovation takes place on many fronts (figure I-1). Product innovations in assembled products—iPods, industrial robots, solar energy–generating arrays—are the type that most often come to mind. But innovation is prevalent in:

- **Technology:** The last several waves of economic growth have been stimulated by technological innovations in different fields: semiconductors (the computer revolution), biotechnology (based on new scientific knowledge), the Internet (the product of a government program), and telecommunications. Innovation in energy technology may be the next big wave.

FIGURE I-1

Innovation on many fronts

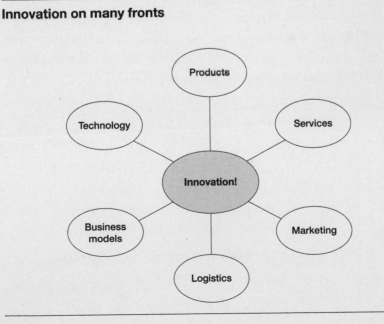

- **Services:** Services now constitute roughly half of the U.S. economy and are fertile ground for innovation. Individuals and pension funds, for example, have invested billions in a dazzlingly varied mutual fund industry that barely existed thirty years ago. That service industry owes much of its success to financial concepts of portfolio management developed at leading schools of business and economics.

- **Processes:** The low manufacturing costs of paints, chemicals, petroleum-based fuels, glass, and countless other nonassembled products and services are the result of continuous process innovation over many years. Assembled goods have likewise benefited from process innovations that have reduced assembly steps and labor costs and improved reliability.

- **Marketing and distribution:** Viral marketing (a technique that uses existing social networks to increase brand awareness), overnight delivery service (FedEx is the notable pioneer), and direct distribution via the Web are all based on innovations in marketing and logistics.

- **Business models:** Apple's approach to generating revenue from iTune downloads of music files, films, and audiobooks rivals Dell's innovative business model in the field of computers and peripherals. Likewise, Amazon's e-book venture, Kindle, represents a new model for generating revenues from text content.

- **Supply chains:** Wal-Mart eclipsed its retail competitors by doing many things right. One of those things was the development of a superefficient supply chain that forged fast and efficient connections between the production facilities of key suppliers with the loading docks of Wal-Mart stores. This just-in-time supply system assures that goods are on the shelf when people want them and eliminates costly stockroom inventories.

But while innovation creates, it can also destroy. More than a half-century ago, economist Joseph Schumpeter described the economic, sociological, and organizational impacts of innovation and its "winds of creative destruction." Those winds sweep away both old ways of doing things and the enterprises and institutions that cling to them. During the nineteenth century, innovations in mass production doomed local shoemakers, dressmakers, and many other artisans. We see that pattern repeated today as "superstores"—a retail innovation—devastate the ranks of small local hardware stores, independent electronic/appliance stores, and office-supply shops. Likewise, innovations in electronics, pharmaceuticals, and other fields—including services—continually undermine established products and services. Enterprises that fail to keep pace with these innovations are quickly swept from the field.

The Innovation Process

Many managers, technical professionals, and scholars see innovation as a process like the one mapped in figure I-2. That process begins with a creative act: recognition of an opportunity. Opportunity recognition often emerges from someone's understanding of a market need. As an executive of the E. Remington and Sons (later the Remington Arms Company) remarked on witnessing a demonstration of a prototype

FIGURE I-2

The innovation process

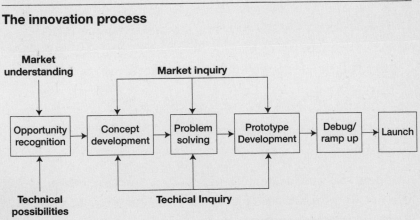

typewriter, "There's an idea that will revolutionize business!" A similar recognition took place when Thomas Edison witnessed the blazing illumination produced by William Wallace's arc lighting system, an impressive but impractical predecessor to the incandescent lamps that Edison would eventually develop. Edison immediately foresaw the commercial potential of electric lighting and launched an intense and tireless effort to exploit it.

Opportunity recognition may also originate from a scientist's or engineer's technical insight. For instance, frustration with conventional thinking about the performance limits of silicon-based semiconductors inspired IBM researcher Bernard Meyerson to experiment with a silicon germanium alloy. The commercial applications of that technology were understood only later.

Once an opportunity is recognized, other process steps follow. The innovative concept must be fleshed out in detail, problems must be solved, and a workable prototype must be developed and tested to the point where it can be evaluated by potential customers. Each of these steps must be enlightened by market/customer and technical understandings.

Decision makers play a role throughout the innovation process, as supporters and as askers of tough questions:

- Will the idea work?

- Does the company have the technical know-how to make it work and the business competencies to make it successful?

- Does the idea represent value for customers?

- Does the idea fit within the framework of company strategy?

- Does it make economic sense for the company?

- Will this innovative project open the door to others or to new markets?

Ideas that produce affirmative answers to these questions and that obtain organizational support are moved further along the road toward market launch. Some make it to the end of that road; most do not. Commercial launch is the final test for innovative ideas. Here, customers make the final evaluation.

Creativity plays a role in the innovation process, though one that is difficult to measure. Creativity sparks the innovative idea and it helps to improve facets of the idea as it moves forward. Creativity is needed on both the technical and market sides of the process. It helps the technologist to see new ways of addressing known customer needs even as it helps customer-facing people find new ways of applying or adapting existing technologies to those needs.

The Challenge to Business Leaders

Unfortunately, top managers seldom play a creative role in the innovation process. Most are too removed from day-to-day customer interactions to be the first to recognize an innovative market opportunity. And, excepting R&D executives, their technical skills may trail behind the cutting edge. Nevertheless, by virtue of their authority to make decisions and to allocate resources, senior leaders are duty-bound to participate in the innovation process. They must stay abreast of technological currents, market insights, and the ideas being debated by their subordinates. Equally important, they must create an organizational climate that encourages experimentation, accepts some level of failure, discourages complacency, and accommodates inventive people who for one reason or another don't quite fit in. Doing all this while tending to day-to-day affairs of the enterprise may be the ultimate challenge of business leadership.

What's Ahead

This book examines the concept of innovation and offers practical suggestions for fostering and aligning it with enterprise strategy. Its content draws on parts of *Managing Creativity and Growth*, an earlier book in the Harvard Business Essentials series, but expands the range of discussion and introduces the strategic issues that every innovator must understand and that every leader must communicate. The book's goal is to make you and your organization more creative and more effective on the all-important innovation front.

As a single volume on a broad topic, *The Innovator's Toolkit* will not make you an expert, but it will give you information you can use to be more effective in stimulating innovation and creativity and capturing their benefits.

Chapter 1 sets the stage with a working definition of innovation and discussion of its different types: incremental and radical; innovations in products, processes, and services. Chapter 2 focuses on innovative ideas. Here you learn where they come from and how you can generate more of them. Chapter 3 is about idea recognition, the Aha! moment when someone sees value in the idea. Just seeing the value of an idea, however, is insufficient; the idea must find support within the organization in order to obtain the resources needed for development. How innovators can gain support is the subject of chapter 4. This naturally leads into chapter 5, which describes practical methods companies can use to pick through the many valuable ideas that come their way and determine which few are worthy of resource support. The pros and cons of the stage-gate system used by many companies are discussed here.

In chapters 6 through 10 the book turns to the strategic issues that relate to innovation. Chapter 6 is a brief primer on business strategy, explaining four typical strategies and how innovation fits into each. Chapter 7 describes several "strategic moves" that you can consider when seeking market entry and commercial success with an innovative concept. Chapters 8 and 9 consider a thinking tool—the S curve—and how business leaders can use it to understand the technological trajectories they are on, alternative trajectories, and whether they should continue along the same path or leap to another S curve.

Early-stage innovations contain elements of risk and potential return. If you're an investor, you probably understand these concepts already. Risk and return are bound together. If you invest in stocks, you probably know enough to diversify—that is, to create a balanced portfolio of many stock issues, some with high-risk/high return characteristics, and others with low-risk/low return characteristics. Leaders of large enterprises will wisely do the same with their innovation projects. Chapter 10 offers practical advice on creating balance portfolios of innovative projects.

The book's final chapters, 11 through 14, are about creativity—the human characteristic that sparks most innovation. What is creativity? How can we recognize it when we see it? What organizational practices encourage or discourage creativity in individuals and groups? What can leaders do to get more of it? The last of these chapters looks at organizational culture, which has so much to do with employee creativity. If culture must change, top management must act. Chapter 14 offers steps they can follow.

Like other books in the Harvard Business Essentials series, this one has useful supplemental material in the back. It features two appendices, a notes section, and a glossary of key terms relating to creativity and innovation. Every discipline has its special vocabulary, and the subject here is no exception. When you see a word italicized in the text, that's your cue that it's defined in the glossary. The final supplement, For Further Reading, identifies books and articles that can tell you more about topics covered in these chapters.

Best of luck with your business and future innovations!

1

Types of Innovation

Several Types on Many Fronts

Key Topics Covered in This Chapter

- *Incremental and radical innovation*

- *Why incremental innovation dominates*

- *Innovation in processes and services*

THE MEANING OF innovation is revealed by its Latin root, *nova*, or new. It is generally understood as the introduction of a new thing or method. Here's a more elaborate definition: *innovation* is the embodiment, combination, and/or synthesis of knowledge in original, relevant, valued new products, processes, or services.

However you define it, innovation takes a number of forms. This chapter will acquaint you with each and help you see how they can help or challenge your business.

Incremental and Radical Innovation

Innovation scholars generally point to two different types of innovation: incremental and radical. ("Other Terms: Sustaining and Disruptive" below provides another way of looking at the different types of innovation.) *Incremental innovation* is generally understood to exploit existing forms or technologies. It either improves on something that already exists or reconfigures an existing form or technology to serve some other purpose. In this sense it is innovation at the margins. For example, Intel's Pentium 4 computer chip represented an incremental innovation over its immediate predecessor, the Pentium 3, since both were based on the same fundamental technology. The Pentium 4 incorporated design improvements and new features

Other Terms: Sustaining and Disruptive

Though the terms *incremental* and *radical* are commonly used to describe the two major forms of innovation, the writing of Harvard professor Clayton Christensen has introduced alternatives and used them in somewhat different ways. Christensen uses the terms *sustaining* and *disruptive* to describe innovations. As he writes: "Some sustaining technologies can be discontinuous or radical in characters, while others are of an incremental nature. What all sustaining technologies have in common is that they improve the performance of established products . . . Most technological advances in a given industry are sustaining in character . . . Disruptive technologies bring to a market a very different value proposition than had been available previously."[a]

In many instances, the disruptive technologies described by Christensen create new markets. Those markets are initially small, but sometimes grow large.

a. Clayton M. Christensen, *The Innovator's Dilemma: When New Technologies Cause Great Firms to Fail* (Boston: Harvard Business School Press, 1997), xv. Christensen develops his sustaining–disruptive concepts in this book and in its sequel (with coauthor Michael E. Raynor), *The Innovator's Solution: Creating and Sustaining Successful Growth* (Boston: Harvard Business School Press, 2003).

that enhanced chip performance. The same can be said for the GPS (global positioning satellite)–based position locators found in many luxury automobiles; these are less innovations than the application of existing GPS technology to a new use (see "Incremental Innovation with a Powerful Twist").

A *radical innovation*, in contrast, is something new to the world and a departure from existing technology or methods. The terms *breakthrough* and *discontinuous* are often used as synonyms for radical innovation. The transistor technology developed at the Bell Labs represented a radical innovation that undermined the electronics industry's dominant players, which at the time were deeply committed to vacuum tube technology. The same could be said for jet propulsion during the 1940s, when piston-powered engines dominated

Incremental Innovation with a Powerful Twist

Earlier, an incremental innovation was defined as one that either improves upon something that already exists or reconfigures an existing form or technology to serve another purpose. Marc Meyer, a professor at Northeastern University, has illuminated the last phrase of that definition in his book, *The Fast Path to Corporate Growth*.[a] Using companies such as IBM, Honda, Mars, and The MathWorks as examples, Meyer describes how companies can leverage their current know-how and technologies to serve new markets and to create new lines of business. The success of the Apple iPod provides rather compelling evidence of this strategy's power. By thinking outside the box of its served market, and by using many of its current technological capabilities, Apple created a new and fast-growing business.

a. Marc H. Meyer, *The Fast Path to Corporate Growth: Leveraging Knowledge and Technologies to New Market Applications* (Oxford/New York: Oxford University Press, 2007).

aviation. Likewise, the silicon-germanium (SiGe) chip technology developed by IBM in the late 1990s represented a radical innovation. SiGe chips had four times the switching power of conventional silicon chips and could operate with much less power, making them ideal for applications in new generations of cell phones, laptop computers, handheld digital devices, and other small, portable devices.[1] Another example of radical innovation is seen in the digital imaging technology used in today's consumer and professional cameras; this represents a radical departure from the chemically coated film technology on which George Eastman built the Eastman Kodak Corporation and the modern photo industry over a century ago. Because of the rapid diffusion of digital imaging—from specialized applications such as satellite earth imaging to amateur photography—photographic film sales have plummeted.

A team of researchers at Rensselaer Polytechnic Institute defined a radical innovation more specifically as an innovation with one or more of the following characteristics:

- An entirely new set of performance features
- Improvements in known performance features of five times or greater, or
- A 30 percent or greater reduction in cost[2]

One could add to this list one of the characteristics cited by Lee A. Sage and the PACE awards program for innovation in the auto supply industry: a change in the basis of competition.[3]

Within industries, incremental and radical innovations go hand in hand. The course of innovation is generally characterized by long periods of incremental innovation punctuated by infrequent radical innovations. For example, in electronics, we observe the introduction of vacuum tubes, which were displaced by transistors, which were in turn largely displaced by the semiconductor. Each of these major transitions represented a great leap forward, but was followed by a period of steady incremental improvements that gradually enhanced performance, lowered cost, and/or reduced size. Figure 1-1 represents a theoretical time line in which radical and incremental improvements take place. Note in this simplified illustration how progress is made through small incremental improvements until radical innovations appear. Progress then takes an abrupt leap forward. Incremental innovation then resumes.

Radical ideas are always in the works somewhere—in R&D labs or in the minds of scientists or entrepreneurs. They usually take a long time to germinate and develop. Their appearance in the marketplace (and few make it to that point) is both infrequent and generally unpredictable. Incremental innovation follows in it train, usually after what Michael Tushman and Charles O'Reilly have called a "period of technological ferment." They use different technologies for keeping time as an example: "During this period of ferment, competing technological variants, each with different operating principles,

FIGURE 1-1

An industry time line of radical and incremental improvement

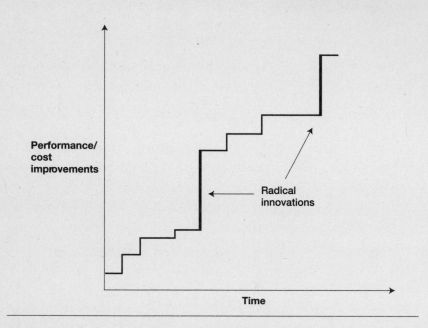

vie for market acceptance. The competition occurs between the existing and the new technology (e.g., between tuning forks, quartz, and escapement oscillation in the watch industry) as well as among variants of that new technology."[4]

These periods of ferment are confusing and uncertain for both producers and customers. In the absence of technical standards, producers don't know which of several new courses to follow (e.g., VHS or Betamax formats; the Mac or DOS/Windows operating systems; HD DVD or Blu-ray). Customers are sometimes paralyzed over the choice of staying with the old technology, switching to the new, or waiting for something even better to come along. Once this period of ferment ends and a dominant technological format emerges, incremental innovation and improvement resumes.

At this point you may find it useful to think about the trajectory of innovation in your own industry. Looking back over the past ten years or so, can you identify innovations that really changed the basis of competition or improved performance in major ways? Which innovations would you describe as radical, and which were clearly incremental? Now look to the present:

- Are you aware of radical innovations now in progress that will impact your industry?

- If and when those innovations enter the marketplace, how will they affect competition?

- How might these innovations impact your own company's sales and profitability?

Factors That Favor Incremental Innovation

Radical innovations have the potential to change the basis of competition in favor of the innovator. For example, IBM's introduction of the electric typewriter signaled the end for all manual typewriter makers in the office market and gave IBM a commanding share of that market for decades. Henry Ford's innovations in automobile design and assembly likewise changed the nature of the emerging auto industry and gave his company a grip on the market that no one would break for over fifteen years. More recently, Wal-Mart's supply chain innovation gave it a major cost advantage over Sears, J.C. Penney, Kmart, and other retail stores, and helped it gain dominance in mass-market retailing. Indeed, there is evidence that the greatest profits and the greatest source of future competitive power are found in radical innovation.[5]

Despite the advantage of radical innovation, it presents companies with several serious challenges. Projects dedicated to radical innovation are risky, expensive, and usually take many years to produce tangible results—if they produce them at all. Research by Leifer and his colleagues on eleven radical innovation R&D projects indicated that at least ten years were required to show tangible results.[6] To be successful, companies must have the patience, determination, and the budgets to support these long timelines. Management and shareholders must be willing to patiently await the future—and lose plenty of sleep along the way.

Radical innovation's association with risk, expense, and long time lines encourages most established companies to pursue incremental innovation, which is safer, cheaper, and more likely to produce results within a reasonable time. By one estimate, 85 to 95 percent of corporate R&D portfolios are made up of incremental projects.[7]

Incremental innovation handled systematically provides business units with the steady streams of new, improved, and varied products and services they need to grow and stay competitive. Incremental innovators must, however, observe two cautions:

1. **Avoid the "more bells and whistles" syndrome:** Pressed by marketers to churn out new versions every few years, many product developers simply add features that few customers really want. This practice irritates many users and creates a future market for true innovators who develop something simpler and more elegant. For example, every new version of office application software suites seems to be bigger, more expensive, and more difficult to master than their predecessors—but offers few tangible benefits for most customers. Customers complain but have few alternatives. Someday, an innovator may provide an alternative that consumes less memory, is competent, less expensive, easier to master, and fully compatible with Microsoft Word, the dominant product. (We may be observing something analogous in the growing success of Linux, which for many is becoming an alternative to the larger, more complex Windows operating system.)

2. **Don't put all of your chips on incremental innovation.** Yes, investments in incremental innovation are less risky and produce results more quickly. But they seldom create a bridge between current and the future generations of technology. Nor will they alter the competitive game sharply in your favor. Only radical innovation can do that. So find a balance in your pursuit of in-

cremental and radical innovations. (Look for more on finding that balance in chapter 10, where portfolio strategy is discussed.) When a game-changing innovation eventually appears, you want it to be one of your own invention.

Process Innovations

People are used to thinking of innovation in terms of physical, manufactured goods such as computer chips, flat-screen displays, fuel cells, night-vision equipment, and so forth. In reality, process innovations are just as important in the competitive life of companies and in industries as diverse as steel, glass, brewing, chemicals, petroleum refining, and paint making.

In many cases, process innovation lowers unit production costs, often by reducing the number of disconnected process steps. In his study of the plate-glass-making industry, James Utterback has provided an illuminating example of how costs can be lowered when innovators find ways to reduce the number of disconnected process steps.[8]

Plate glass was traditionally produced through a series of separate steps: mixing and melting the ingredients in a furnace; casting a glass ingot in a mold; annealing the ingot in a special oven; and, finally, grinding and polishing the ingot using successively finer abrasives. This process was slow, labor- and energy-intensive, and very expensive. Over the years, innovators in the glass industry found ways to integrate or mechanize various steps, thus increasing throughput time and reducing unit cost.

The ultimate glassmaking innovation, however, was the "float glass" process introduced by U.K.-based Pilkington Glass in the 1960s. That process, the result of ten years of thinking, experimenting, and debugging, integrated all the tasks of glassmaking into a single automated step. Raw materials poured into a furnace at one end became a continuous ribbon of molten glass that, after passing through an annealing oven, emerged as a flawlessly smooth finished product at the

other end. The costly grinding and polishing steps were entirely eliminated. Pilkington's innovation so reduced the cost of production that
the float glass process quickly displaced all other approaches, giving the
company a major competitive advantage for many years.

The Product–Process Connection

It's one thing to create an innovative new product or service; it's another thing to create a process capable of manufacturing or delivering the new product/service at a price the target market will accept.
Thus, innovation in both realms is often connected, and some innovative product ideas must await process innovation before they can
achieve market traction.

The product-process connection is nicely illustrated in the case
of the now-ubiquitous disposable baby diaper. Versions of this product first appeared in North America in the mid-1950s, during the
postwar baby boom, when the market for this product was huge and
growing. Nevertheless, these early disposables failed to gain more
than a 1 percent market share. The reason was twofold: poor performance and price.

When Cincinnati-based Procter & Gamble entered the field, its
R&D people very quickly solved the performance problem by using
more suitable materials and a new design. That was the easy part.
Developing a cost-effective process for manufacturing its new diaper
proved to be a far greater challenge, and one that held back market
rollout for longer than anticipated. One engineer described P&G's
quest for an effective diapermaking process as the most complex operation the company had ever faced.[9] Their problem was finding a
way to manufacture this multipart, multimaterial product in huge
quantities at a price acceptable to customers. The company encountered a similar problem years later when it attempted to develop its
ersatz potato chip, Pringles. Here again, the product idea was com-
paratively simple and straightforward; developing an extrusion and
baking process that would produce high volumes of very thin, stack-
able, and uniformly cooked "chips" proved to be the real challenge.

Service Innovations

Service is another area in which innovation plays a key role. Service innovation sometimes produces winning business models. Here are a few notable examples:

- **Dell:** Dell's PCs are very good, but they share the same technologies as machines offered by competitors. What originally set this company apart and gave it a competitive edge was not its product, but its innovative strategy of skipping the middleman and selling custom-configured PCs directly to buyers. Later innovations in supply chain management made this strategy fast and effective—and helped to make Dell the world's most successful PC manufacturer.

- **Southwest Airlines:** Herb Kelleher and his associates built this popular and profitable business through an innovative value proposition to customers: low fares, frequent service, and fun. Kelleher initially developed his service concept to compete with automobile and bus transportation in the Texas regional market. It succeeded there and was expanded, eventually making Southwest the most profitable airline in the United States.

- **Zipcar:** This young company has created an alternative to automobile ownership for urban dwellers in more than a dozen U.S. cities, as well as London and Toronto. Its mission is to offer members affordable twenty-four-hour access to vehicles for short-term round-trips. A member who needs a car for an occasional drive to the suburbs or for weekly grocery hauling reserves one on the company Web site, goes to one of the many locations where Zipcars are parked, unlocks the vehicle with a Zipcard, and drives away. Payment is based on time and mileage. By early 2008, the company had over thirty-five hundred vehicles and more than 300,000 subscribers ("Zipsters").

Thus, innovation is not the sole domain of physical product companies. Many service-driven companies have long and admirable histories of innovation. But not every service innovator succeeds.

Consider the fate of Streamline.com, a Boston-based company whose business model aimed to provide cost-effective, high-quality home delivery of groceries, dry cleaning, prepared meals, shoe repair, and many other household items. It was a great concept, and its inventors supported it with Internet connectivity, a fleet of delivery vans, and a state-of-the-art distribution center. But for all its appeal, Steamline went bankrupt. So did Webvan, an even more ambitious enterprise using a similar business model. In both cases, the service idea was appealing, but the process for delivering value to customer doorsteps either failed or proved too costly. One competitor, Peapod, currently a unit of Royal Ahold, has survived and prospered since its founding in 1989. As of 2008 it was providing online grocery shopping services to customers in many U.S. metropolitan areas in partnership with Royal Ahold's two major American supermarket chains: Stop & Shop and Giant Food.

So if you've developed an appealing innovation service concept, your job has only begun. Give as much or more attention to the process and the infrastructure needed to support it. Think carefully about every step that goes into the production and delivery of your service. Then try to think of how each could be improved (incrementally), combined, or replaced entirely (radically) by something better, faster, and less costly.

Summing Up

This chapter began with a working definition of innovation—as the embodiment, combination, and/or synthesis of knowledge in original, relevant, valued new products, processes, or services. It went on to describe the two major categories within which innovations fall: incremental and radical.

- Incremental innovation exploits existing forms or technologies. It either improves something that already exists, making it "new and improved," or reconfigures an existing form or technology to serve some other purpose. The GPS position locators found in many luxury automobiles is an example of an existing technology adapted to a different purpose.

- A radical innovation was described as something new to the world. Many radical innovations have the potential to displace established technologies (as the transistor did when first introduced into the world of vacuum tubes) or create entirely new markets.

- When compared with radical innovation, incremental innovation takes less time and involves less risk, which explains why managers favor it. Incremental innovation alone, however, cannot assure a company's future competitiveness.

- Radical and incremental innovations often operate hand in hand. Thus, the introduction of a successful radical innovation is often followed by a period of incremental innovations, which improve its performance or extend its application.

The chapter went on to underscore the importance of process innovations, which are often overlooked.

- Process innovations generally aim to achieve substantial reductions in unit costs of production or service delivery. In many cases this is accomplished by integrating or eliminating separate process steps.

- Product and process innovations often go hand in hand. As demonstrated by the case of the disposable baby diaper; a breakthrough product often fails to gain market acceptance until a low-cost process for manufacturing it at acceptable quality levels is created.

Finally, service innovations, as exemplified by Southwest Airlines, Dell, and Zipcar, were examined. Service innovators are urged to think carefully about the processes that support production and delivery of their services.

2

Idea Generation

Innovation's Starting Point

Key Topics Covered in This Chapter

- *New knowledge as a source of innovation*

- *Tapping the ideas of customers*

- *Learning from lead users*

- *Empathetic design*

- *Invention factories and skunkworks*

- *Open market innovation*

- *The role of mental preparation*

- *How management can encourage idea generation*

- *Idea-generating techniques*

INNOVATIVE IDEAS HAVE many sources. Some originate in a flash of inspiration. Others are accidental. But as Peter Drucker told readers of *Harvard Business Review* almost two decades ago, most result from a conscious, purposeful search for opportunities to solve problems or please customers.[1] His observation supports Thomas Edison's famous statement that invention is 1 percent inspiration and 99 percent perspiration.

Ideas are essential building blocks from which innovation and innovative technologies and products are made. By one estimate, it takes three thousand of them to produce a single commercial success.[2] Given that ratio, companies must regularly generate many ideas.

This chapter examines six sources of innovative ideas: new knowledge, customers, lead users, empathetic design, invention factories and skunkworks, and the open market of idea. It goes on to discuss the important role of mental preparation, and what management can do to generate more good ideas.

New Knowledge

Many, if not most, radical innovations are the product of new knowledge. Consider the computer, the product of new knowledge in the areas of binary mathematics, symbolic logic, programming concepts, and various technological breakthroughs, including the audion electronic switch. New knowledge developed by Francis

Crick and James Watson in the early 1950s on the structure of the DNA molecule opened the door to innovations in medicine, agriculture, and animal husbandry. Likewise, IBM's innovative silicon-germanium chip resulted from laboratory findings that contradicted accepted wisdom on certain properties of that alloy. The SiGe chip has now found important new uses in electronic devices where processing speed and low power consumption are critically important.

Corning, Inc., whose roots go back to the late nineteenth century, provides one of the best examples of a company that has survived and prospered on market applications developed from new knowledge, most of it generated within its own laboratories. Citing a series of landmark innovations in materials—glass lightbulbs, heat-resistant Pyrex glass, television tubes, extruded honeycomb ceramics for catalytic converters, and fiber optics—Corning Research Fellow George Beall told an audience of industrial R&D members that "the development of landmark new products at Corning has been almost always dependent on knowledge gleaned from previous exploratory research."[3]

While innovations based on new knowledge are often powerful, there is generally a lengthy time delay between development of new knowledge and its transformation into commercially viable products and services. The computer took over fifty years to surface in the market. Satellite communications took even longer. Considering all the elements that are required to launch and maintain earth satellites—knowledge of calculus, physics, electronics, and aeronautical science—we can say that the timeline of satellite communications stretches back several hundred years to Newton and Kepler.

Despite the time lags involved with knowledge-based innovation, the rewards are often enormous. Consider Corning's development of fiber optics technology, which that company now dominates. Corning scientists began learning about the light-transmitting properties of glass "light pipes" in 1966, but it wasn't until 1970 that a team of company scientists produced a material capable of transmitting electronic impulses at the levels required by standards of the day. It took many more years for the new material to find a place in the market.

Customer Ideas

Customers are an evergreen source of innovative ideas *if* salespeople, service personnel, market researchers, and R&D workers listen to what customers say and probe for more. Customers, for example are often the best source of information on the weaknesses of current products: "It's a great device, and I'd use it more often if it would fit in my briefcase." (*Idea:* Make a smaller version of the device).

Customers can also be the best source for identifying unsolved problems: "Our pizza restaurant chain has never been able to generate much lunchtime business. It takes too long to prepare and bake a regular pizza." (*Idea 1:* Develop an oven capable of cutting the cooking time in half; *idea 2:* Develop a half-prepared pizza product.)

Most companies appreciate the importance of customers as a source of new ideas, and they mine that source regularly through market research. You should also. When quizzing customers, however, be less concerned with product or service specifications and more concerned with the *outcomes* that customers seek. This is the advice of consultant Anthony Ulwick, founder of Strategyn. Using the example of music storage media, the preferred outcomes would be "access to a large number of songs, play without distortion over time, resist damage during normal use, and require minimal storage space. These are outcomes, not solutions."[4] The next step, according to Ulwick, is to prioritize the list of desired outcomes according to their importance to customers, with each outcome being quantified. For example, research might indicate that "play without distortion" is the most important value, and "resist damage" is the least important.

Direct Customer Participation

Companies have typically depended on formal market research, focus groups, and routine contacts through sales personnel to tap the ideas of customers. Today, some companies are actively inviting customers to share their ideas via the Internet, producing what some call the "democratization" of innovation. Consider the case of Starbucks. Disappointing business results in late 2007 and early 2008 motivated this company to scramble for ways to regenerate growth. One response was "My Starbucks Idea," which invites customers to share their ideas for improving Starbucks's products, the customer experience, and the corporation's community involvement. In this program, customers describe their ideas via the company Web site. Other customers have an opportunity to vote on the merits on those ideas and leave written comments. Those votes and comments are viewable by all site visitors. The company also tells visitors how it is responding to the most popular ideas.

Consider the following example from the My Starbucks Idea program, as described on its Web site. In late March 2008, a customer offered this suggestion: "Develop a means whereby someone can purchase a gift Starbucks drink for a friend or coworker via the Internet. The company would then send an e-mail to the gift recipient with a message ('Katie has bought you a drink!') and a printable bar-coded certificate redeemable at any Starbucks coffee shop."

Within ten weeks, according to the Starbucks site, sixteen hundred people had voted in favor of this idea and 104 had submitted written comments on why it was a good or bad idea, how the idea could be improved, and so forth.

The Starbucks program garnered more than sixteen thousand ideas from customers within the first few months of operation. During that time, several customer ideas were implemented (e.g., the Starbucks Energy Drink), and a great many more were under review by management. The potential of this type of democratized idea generation is substantial, and the ability of customers to vote on the merits of submitted ideas provides an inexpensive measure of market testing. Best of all, this method is ongoing, costs very little to implement and maintain, and no doubt builds some level of customer identification with the company, its products, and its well-being.

SAS, one of the world's most successful software companies, likewise taps into its customer base to gather ideas. Every day it gathers—and acts on—customer complaints and suggestions obtained through its Web site, over the telephone, and through an annual user conference. Customer input is prioritized and routed to appropriate SAS experts for evaluation and action. The company estimates that

Google's $10 Million Contest

Like Starbucks, Google has turned to the public for ideas. In 2007, the company announced its plan to develop a mobile phone capable of challenging the Apple iPhone and other contenders. The plan is to base the new device on the "Android" software platform and operating system. This open system allows allied developers to contribute. Some thirty-four companies were involved in the alliance in 2007.

Eager to tap the creativity of the software development community, Google announced the Android Developer Challenge in November 2007, and offered $10 million in prize money to encourage participation. Under the terms of the challenge, submitters of the fifty most promising applications would each be given $25,000 to continue development. Those fifty projects would be reduced to twenty at a later date, and those survivors would receive even higher payments to continue development.

To cash-rich Google, the Android Developer Challenge was an inexpensive technique to quickly attract independent ideas for creating what might become a multibillion-dollar new business.

80 percent of customer requests are acted on. ("Google's $10 Million Contest" profiles another company that tapped customers for innovative ideas.)

Beware the Tyranny of Served Markets

Observe one caution in listening to customers: they are capable of diverting you from your pursuit of real innovation. If that sounds counterintuitive, consider this. Good businesspeople take the virtue of listening to customers and pleasing them as an article of faith. But sticking too closely to current customers can stifle innovation and lock your company into technologies that have no future. This happens when (1) customers fail to understand technical possibilities, and (2) when they are afraid that real innovations will render their current systems obsolete. Consider these related examples:

- Market researchers ask a customer focus group to describe the kind of automobile they would like to purchase five years in the future. With limited knowledge of alternative technical possibilities, and with current autos as their only reference point, the focus group describes a vehicle very similar to those currently in the showrooms.

- A customer has recently purchased a $10 million hardware and software system from your company. When queried about new ideas, this customer does not encourage you to create anything that might undermine the value of that investment—such as a new operating system. Instead, you'll be encouraged to incrementally improve the current system.

Some companies compound the "tyranny of served markets" described in the second example by creating review systems that kill ideas and products that their current customers do not want. They focus all their resources on serving today's profitable customers and markets. This almost guarantees that they will produce nothing but slightly improved versions of their current products and services and will surely miss the next big wave of change that alters the competitive environment.

Learning from Lead Users

Lead users are another valuable source of potentially innovative ideas. Some studies show that between 10 percent and 40 percent of product users modify off-the-shelf products or develop others that fill their particular needs. *Lead users* are companies and individuals—both customers and noncustomers—whose needs are far ahead of market trends. They may be pioneering radiologists searching for better ways to produce diagnostic images. They may be military pilots, professional athletes, or mining engineers who modify off-the-shelf equipment to achieve higher effectiveness in the field. In all cases, their needs motivate them to produce innovations that suit their unique requirements—long before manufacturers think of them.

Lead users are seldom interested in commercializing their innovations. Instead, they innovate for their own purposes because existing products fail to meet their needs. And a surprising number of them will freely reveal the nature of their innovations to others. Open source software is an example of the willingness of user-innovators to share their advances. Those innovations can often be adapted to the needs of larger markets.

MIT professor Eric Von Hippel was the first to study lead users as a source of innovative ideas. In several of the fields he studied—notably scientific instruments, semiconductors, and computers—more than half of all innovations were made by users, not by product manufacturers. Thus, approaching these lead users and studying their unique applications and product modifications can effectively augment internal idea generation. As an example, Von Hippel suggests that an automotive brake manufacturer might seek out particular users whose requirements for effective breaking exceed those of normal users. These might be auto racing teams, producers of military aircraft, or manufacturers of heavy trucks.

In most cases, the discovery of a user innovation by a manufacturer is accidental—for example, the result of a field sales representative's visit to a customer site. More systematic exploitation of user-generated innovation can produce much better results. Von Hippel cites research showing that 3M's forecasted annual sales of lead user–generated ideas were conservatively estimated to be more than eight times those forecasted for new products developed in the usual 3M manner (see "A Four-Phase Process"). More important, lead user–generated projects were found to create ideas for new product lines, while traditional market-research methods were more likely to produce incremental improvements to existing lines of business.[5]

A Four-Phase Process

An article coauthored by Eric Von Hippel, Stefan Thomke, and Mary Sonnack described a four-phase process used by some 3M units to glean innovative ideas from lead users. This may work for you.

1. **Lay the foundation:** Identify the targeted markets and the type and level of innovations desired by the organization's key stakeholders. These stakeholders must be on board early.

2. **Determine the trends:** Talk to experts in the field about what they see as the important trends. These experts are people who have a broad view of emerging technologies and leading-edge application in the area being studied.

3. **Identify and learn from the lead users:** Use networking to identify users at the leading edge of the target market and related markets. Develop relationships with these lead users and gather information from them that points to break-through products. Use this learning to shape preliminary product ideas and assess their business potential.

4. **Develop breakthroughs:** The goal of this phase is to move preliminary concepts toward completion. Host two- to three-day workshops with several lead users, a small group of in-house marketing and technical people, and the lead user investigative team. Work in small groups, then as a whole, to design final concepts.

SOURCE: Adapted from Eric Von Hippel, Stefan Thomke, and Mary Sonnack, "Creating Breakthroughs at 3M," *Harvard Business Review*, September–October 1999, 47–57.

Empathetic Design

As noted earlier, one of the problems that innovators face in determining market needs is that target customers cannot always recognize or articulate their future needs. Because most are unaware of technical possibilities, they tend to identify their needs in terms of current products and services with which they are already familiar. They express their needs in terms of incremental improvements to these products and services: a thinner laptop, an automobile with better fuel economy, a TV screen with better resolution, faster service. To generate innovations that go beyond incremental improvements, you must identify needs and solve problems that customers may not yet recognize. Empathetic design is a technique for doing this. *Empathetic design* is an idea-generating technique whereby innovators observe how people use existing products and services in their own environments. Harley-Davidson has used this technique, sending engineers, marketing personnel, and even social anthropologists to HOG (Harley Owners Group) events. These employees observed how Harley owners use and customize their bikes, the problems they encounter using Harley products, and so forth. The company has taken this ethnography approach a step further by sponsoring periodic "Posse Rides" that bring company managers and Harley owners together in 2,300-mile road trips from South Padre Island, Texas, to the Canadian border. These long treks give company participants opportunities to build relationships with customers in a relaxed setting and to observe their likes, dislikes, and biking aspirations.[6] Those observations became the raw materials for innovative ideas. Following this same strategy, a Japanese consumer electronics company sent a young engineer to live with an American family for six months to observe how they cooked their meals, communicated with friends, and entertained themselves. Those observations were used in the design of new consumer products.

Some companies take this approach very seriously. IDEO, a leading product design company, bases its design process on an anthropologic approach. Its cofounder, David Kelley, has described some of the things he looks for when he makes a deep dive into the customer world—what people care about, what frustrates them in using current products or services. He watches for smiles or frowns.[7]

Author/professor Marc Meyer has described how Honda used this same approach in the design of its popular Element SUV. Initially conceived to address the mobility needs of a demographic group for which the company had no uniquely designed vehicle (eighteen- to twenty-six-year-old U.S. males), members of the development team went to college fraternity houses to talk with young men about their transportation-related activities—going to beach, hauling bikes and surfboards to outings, moving furniture between apartments, socializing, etc. They even brought together design team members, a small focus group, and several Honda executives for a weekend campout on a California beach. Through these and other avenues of inquiry, the development team learned that their young male target market needed a spacious interior for stowing gear, large back and side doors for getting gear and people in and out, and, of course, a powerful sound system. They also needed a cargo-area floor that was flat and easy to sweep out, and scratch-resistant exterior body panels. Models and sketches developed by the design team were shared with "the guys" to obtain feedback.

The resulting vehicle incorporated features that accommodated the lifestyles of eighteen- to twenty-six-year-old men at a reasonable price. First-year sales of the Element were twice what Honda had anticipated. To the company's delight, many buyers were men and women in their thirties, forties, and fifties who shared one thing with the initial target audience: an active lifestyle.[8]

Procter & Gamble, a prolific new-product producer, is another user of empathetic design. It trains all new R&D personnel in what it calls "Product Research," P&G's approach to observing how customers use products in their day-to-day lives. The program's goal is to put people who have knowledge of technical possibilities and design in direct contact with the world experienced by potential customers. As described by Dorothy Leonard and Jeffrey Rayport, empathetic design is a five-step process:[9]

1. **Observe:** As described above, company representatives observe people using products in their home and workplaces. The key questions in this step are: who should be observed, and who should do the observing?

2. **Capture data:** Observers should capture data on what people are doing, why they are doing it, and the problems they encounter.

Since much of the data is visual and nonquantifiable, use photo-graphs, videos, and drawings to capture the data.

3. **Reflection and analysis:** In this step, observers return from the field and share their experiences with colleagues. Reflection and analysis may result in returning people to the field to gather more data.

4. **Brainstorm:** This step is used to transform observations into graphic representations of possible solutions.

5. **Develop solution prototypes:** Prototypes clarify new concepts, allow others to interact with them, and can be used to stimulate the reactions of potential customers. Are potential customers attracted by the prototypes? What alterations do they suggest?

As the reader can easily imagine, empathetic design is especially important when developing consumer products for nondomestic markets, where preferences for product size, colors, and applications may be very different than those preferred by the home market.

Invention Factories and Skunkworks

Many large manufacturers generate and develop innovative ideas through formal research and development (R&D) units—innovation factories, if you will ("The Wizard's Invention Factory" discusses the granddaddy of them all). Some enterprises support R&D at two levels: the corporate level and the business-unit level. Generally, corporate-level R&D works on radical innovations and enabling technologies that various operating units can use. Bell Labs, a research arm of Alcatel-Lucent, provides an example. Since its founding in 1925 as an R&D center for Bell Telephone, Bell Labs has produced a stream of scientific and technological breakthroughs, including sound-synchronous motion pictures, the transistor, long-distance television transmission, digital cell phone technology, the

The Wizard's Invention Factory

Today we are used to idea of corporate and university research centers—well-equipped and funded laboratories where teams of scientists and technicians conduct research and development on tomorrow's breakthrough technologies. Nothing like this existed, however, until the late 1800s, when Thomas Edison systematized the business of innovation.

Edison set up his first R&D center in Menlo Park, New Jersey, in 1876 with the goal of developing technologies and inventions with commercialization potential. As a way of pursuing innovation, this was itself an innovation. Using his earnings from previous inventions (such as the stock ticker) and investors' capital, he set up shop in a facility that included a long two-story clapboard building, a smaller brick mechanical shop, some small sheds, and a farmhouse. He stocked these buildings with technical books, machining equipment, laboratory instruments, electrical testing devices, chemicals, and staffed them with more than forty capable mechanics and technicians.

Within five years, Edison had outgrown Menlo Park and moved to a larger facility in West Orange, New Jersey. But during that short period he and his associates had patented four hundred inventions and churned out a number of important commercial successes (as well as some spectacular failures), including the carbon transmitter for the Bell telephone, the phonograph, the tasimeter (a supersensitive heat-measuring device), and the incandescent electric lamp. And Thomas Edison became known as "the Wizard of Menlo Park." More important, Menlo Park created a model for modern industrial research.

SOURCE: Adapted with permission from James M. Utterback, *Mastering the Dynamics of Innovation: How Companies Can Seize Opportunities in the Face of Technological Change* (Boston: Harvard Business School Press, 1994), 59–60.

wireless local area network, and the Unix computer operating system. Our world would be notably different absent innovations spawned in this invention factory, which has a twofold mission:

- Conduct basic research in scientific fields related to communications

- Develop leading-edge products and services

This mission is typical of corporate-level R&D, which is heavily focused on radical innovation. R&D at the business-unit level, in contrast, generally focuses on incremental projects that will benefit the units directly and in the short-term. Business-unit managers with profit-and-loss responsibilities are either unable or unwilling to shoulder the financial burden of long-term radical innovation projects. They look to corporate R&D for those.

In their study of eleven radical innovation projects, Richard Leifer and his colleagues found that business units were happy to accept a radical innovation hand-off from corporate R&D labs, but only *after* most of the expensive and time-consuming work had been done.[10] The aim of these managers was to improve the performance of the mainstream business—which usually means a focus on incremental innovation.

A formal R&D program is not the only structure for creating innovative ideas. Some companies have generated and developed ideas by temporarily bringing together talented people with different perspectives with the sole purpose of solving a particular problem. ("Idea Contests" shows one way organizations get innovative ideas from within their ranks.) In some cases, these individuals are located in remote or isolated settings to keep team members focused on their mission, to minimize interference from the rest of the organization, provide autonomy, or to maintain secrecy. The term *skunkworks* is often applied to these focused project teams. The term was first coined in 1943 by Lockheed Aircraft Corporation (now Lockheed Martin) to describe the project center it used to develop the first U.S. fighter jet, the XP-80. Lee Sage has described a similar situation at Johnson Controls, Inc. (JCI), a major supplier of vehicle interiors

Idea Contests

Most business students are familiar with business plan contests. Individual students or student teams create ideas for new start-up businesses. They develop these into formal business plans and submit them to a panel of professors and local venture capitalists. These contests are good practice for would-be entrepreneurs. Better still, the top plans are rewarded with cash prizes—seed money with which to develop their ideas into real businesses.

This same contest concept has been applied in corporations to generate ideas with commercial potential. The Corporate Technology department of Siemens carried out one of these contests in 1996 as part of a companywide innovation initiative. Fourteen hundred Siemens employees in Europe and the United States participated. Here's how it worked: the company put out a call for innovative ideas for new products, processes, services, and systems that could be realized in two or three years. No basic research ideas were allowed. Ideas submitted for the contest could be for new businesses or enhancements to old ones. Within four months, 245 ideas had been submitted. These were screened by a jury of eighteen experts who collaborated with appropriate business units. Forty-six ideas survived this jury "stage gate" and went to personal presentations to senior management, which selected six finalists. All finalists received seed money with which to develop their ideas further.

SOURCE: Jörg Schepers, Ralf Schnell, and Pat Vroom, "From Idea to Business—How Siemens Bridges the Innovation Gap," *Research-Technology Management* 42, no. 3 (May–June 1999): 26–31.

to the auto industry. Besides its corporate mission, JCI had a dual goal of using more recycled materials and producing zero landfill wastes. To further that goal, it wanted to create a new material for its products, and chose to do so through a skunkworks project. As told by Sage: "[T]he company identified 30 engineers it viewed as competent and creative in the materials area, set them up in an unused company building in Holland, Michigan, and asked them to come up with a new and suitable car interior material. . . ."[11]

JCI's skunkworks eventually produced CorteX, an energy-absorbing material made from recycled plastic soft-drink bottles and carpeting. CorteX found its way into vehicle overhead systems, door panels, and other auto interior features developed by the company. This idea-generation experience was so successful that JCI adopted it again—this time for a one-year project to create innovations in vehicle seats.

Tips on Where to Look for Innovative Ideas

Are you having trouble finding innovative ideas for your business? Every one of the ideas sources described in this chapter can help you. Other places to look include:

- **Wherever a new technology and customer needs intersect:** Global positioning satellite (GPS) technology was developed for military navigation. This technology and the need of auto drivers to know their locations relative to destinations created a new product option on luxury automobiles. Within just a few years it had become a standard feature.

- **Either–or propositions:** Remember when manufacturers told us that we could either have high quality or low price—but not both? Remember when carmakers said that we could either have a large fuel guzzler or a tiny fuel-efficient vehicle? Each of these either–or propositions crumbled as innovators found opportunities within what proved to be false assumptions. What either–or propositions are limiting the choices of your customers today?

- **Demographic change:** Aging populations in North America; Europe; and Japan, South Korea, and some other Asian countries have created opportunities for applying existing technology to new uses. In the United States, for instance, this demographic shift has prompted some home builders to examine how they design kitchens, bathrooms, and closets from the perspective of older residents who may have trouble reaching high shelves, negotiating steps, and getting in and out of showers. Innovations in the cosmetic surgery, pharmaceuticals (think Viagra), dental implants, replacement heart valves, and bone-anchored micro hearing aids have all emerged in the shadow of a substantial demographic change.

- **Market change:** The big Wall Street firms laughed when Charles Schwab created his no-frills discount brokerage service. Schwab correctly recognized that more and more successful baby boomers were developing nest eggs and looking for places to put them. His do-it-yourself brokerage service appealed to many of these affluent boomers.

- **Fundamental pricing shifts:** The rising price of oil—coupled with the threat of global warming—has catalyzed an unprecedented level of research and practical innovation, confirming a general understanding that innovation is most likely to occur where the rewards of innovation are greatest. The rapid escalation in petroleum prices, from $20 per barrel in May 1999 to $146 in the summer of 2008, was a disaster for airlines, trucking companies, makers of gas-guzzling SUVs, and everyone else whose business model depended on low-cost oil. But that huge pricing shift produced opportunities for innovators in transportation, alternative energy production, lighting, residential and commercial construction, and countless other fields. That period witnessed the introduction of energy-saving LED and compact florescent lights, the Honda/Climate Energy Freewatt hybrid home heating/electricity-generating system, cleaner diesel engines, concentrated solar power electric generation, and thousands of other breakthroughs.

Open Market Innovation

Not everything must be "invented here." Innovative ideas can often be acquired (or sold) in the open market. Bain & Company's Darrell Rigby and Chris Zook coined the term *open market innovation* in describing how companies can reach outside for the ideas they need for new products and services. As described by Rigby and Zook in a *Harvard Business Review* article, open market innovation employs licensing, joint ventures, and strategic alliances to bring the benefits of free trade to the flow of new ideas.[12] For example, confronted with the anthrax scare that first hit the United States in late 2001, Pitney Bowes—a major producer of mail metering systems—had no ideas about how to help customer organizations whose mail put employees at risk. Needing ideas and solutions fast, it looked outside for help. With the collaboration of outside inventors, it quickly developed scanning and imaging technologies capable of spotting contaminated letters and package.

As described by Rigby and Zook, open-market innovation has four distinct advantages:

1. Importing new ideas can help you multiply the "building blocks" of innovation.

2. Exporting ideas is a good way to raise cash and keep talent.

3. Exporting ideas gives companies a way to measure an innovation's real value.

4. Exporting and importing ideas helps companies clarify what they do best.[13]

There are, of course, risks associated with collaborating across organizational boundaries. Key among them is the danger of failing to adequately capitalize on ideas shared with others in the open market. The best safeguard against this danger is a deal structure that protects your interests.

Open market innovation can also tap the creativity of suppliers, university and government labs, and other sources through what

Larry Huston and Nabil Sakkab call the "connect and develop" method. As they explained in a 2006 article on this subject, Procter & Gamble had innovated for decades from within, employing global research facilities staffed by some of the best talent.[14] In 2000, management saw the need for a new approach; it dispensed with the company's age-old "invent it ourselves" approach to innovation and embraced a "connect and develop" model. By identifying promising ideas throughout the world and applying its own capabilities to them, P&G realized it could create better and cheaper products, faster. The result is that the company now collaborates with suppliers, competitors, scientists, entrepreneurs, and others (that's the connect part). It systematically scours the world for proven technologies, packages, and products that P&G can improve, scale up, and market, either on its own or in partnership with other companies. Thanks in part to this approach, R&D productivity at Procter & Gamble increased by nearly 60 percent. As described by Huston and Sakkab, P&G launched more than one hundred new products in 2004 and 2005 for which some aspect of development came from outside the company.

If you adopt this method, consider this advice:

- **First, identify consumer needs:** Clarify what you're looking for before you begin scouring the world for ideas. Ask business-unit leaders which consumer needs, when satisfied, will drive their brands' growth. Translate needs into briefs describing problems to solve. Consider where you might seek solutions. For example, P&G unit managers identified a need for laundry detergent that cleans effectively in cold water. They decided to search for relevant innovations in chemistry and biotechnology solutions that enable products to work well at low temperatures. Possibilities included labs studying enzymatic reactions in microbes that thrive under polar caps.

- **Identify adjacencies:** Ask which new product categories, related to your current categories, can enhance your existing brand equity. Then seek innovative ideas in those categories. For example, P&G expanded its Crest brand beyond toothpaste to include whitening strips, power toothbrushes, and flosses.

- **Leverage your networks:** Cultivate both proprietary and open networks whose members may have promising ideas. P&G's proprietary networks, for example, include its top fifteen suppliers, who collectively have fifty thousand R&D staff. P&G created a secure IT platform to share problem briefs with these suppliers—who can't see others' responses to briefs. P&G's open networks include NineSigma, a company that connects interested corporations with universities, government and private labs, and consultants that can develop solutions to science and technology problems. NineSigma creates briefs describing contracting companies' problems and sends them to thousands of possible solution providers worldwide.

- **Distribute and screen ideas:** Once you have identified ideas for refining and further commercializing existing products or for employing technology solutions to create new products, distribute those ideas internally—ensuring that managers screen them for potential. For example, at P&G, product ideas are logged on P&G's online "eureka catalog" through a template that documents pertinent facts—such as current sales of existing products or patent availability for a new technology. The document goes to P&G general managers, brand managers, and R&D teams worldwide. Product ideas are also promoted to relevant business-line managers, who gauge their business potential and identify possible obstacles to development.

The Role of Mental Preparation

Many ideas are generated unintentionally through random observations, routine contacts with customers, and even unintended laboratory results. However, to quote Louis Pasteur, "Chance favors the prepared mind." A prepared mind is more likely to formulate a problem-solving idea or recognize an opportunity.

The value of a prepared mind is underscored by the invention of 3M's fabric protector, Scotchgard, a development triggered by a 1953 laboratory accident. Researcher Patsy Sherman was conducting

Tips for Developing Innovative Ideas

Authors Scott Anthony, Matt Eyring, and Lib Gibson offer the following tips for seeking opportunities for disruptive, or industry-altering, innovative ideas:

- **Make it easier and simpler for people to get important jobs done:** Look for people who are frustrated by jobs they must do. For example, many people were frustrated when they had to wait several days to receive an important repair part, a notarized document, or some other item in order to complete their work. Overnight express delivery (e.g., FedEx), has solved that problem for millions each day.

- **Find ways to prosper at the low end of an established market:** Not everyone needs or can afford the level of performance offered by successful, established products. This is particularly true for people in low-income economies. The LifeStraw, a simple $2 item, has given the estimated one billion people who lack access to clean drinking water a low-cost way to obtain safe water without spending large sums on more advanced, electricity-dependent systems. The success of micro lending—i.e., lending sums as little as $100 to entrepreneurs in third-world countries—provides a similar example.

- **Remove barriers to consumption:** Some products and services can be obtained only through expensive intermediaries. For example, not long ago, a woman who wanted to know if she was pregnant had to make an appointment and have a test done at a clinic or doctor's office. Today, she can do the test herself with an easy-to-use, low-cost kit available at any pharmacy. A lack of skills can also be a barrier to consumption. Intuit discovered this problem with existing small business accounting and bookkeeping software. Lacking skills, many small business owners had no choice but to hire professionals. Intuit lowered the skills barrier when it developed its hugely successful QuickBooks product.

SOURCE: Scott Anthony, Matt Eyring, and Lib Gibson, "Mapping Your Innovation Strategy," *Harvard Business Review*, May 2006.

fluorochemical polymer experiments when a lab assistant accidentally spilled some of the solution on her tennis shoes. Sherman tried
to remove it using soap and water, alcohol, and other solvents, but
nothing worked. As often happens in cases where the people involved have technical training, keen powers of observation, and na-
tive curiosity, a light went on in Sherman's mind. She reasoned that
if the substance was impervious to solvents and other substances, it
also might protect textiles from stains. Further development of the
substance led to a successful new product.

Preparation is often cited as the first step in the creative process
that leads to innovation. To prepare themselves for idea generation,
would-be innovators should immerse themselves in the problem at
hand. According to an article by Arthur Shapero, an expert on managing creativity, they should:

- Search the literature

- Look at all sides of the problem

- Talk with people who are familiar with the problem

- Play with the problem

- Ignore the accepted wisdom[15]

How Management Can Encourage
Idea Generation

If innovation is a key function of companies, then management has
a responsibility to encourage the generation of innovative ideas.
Both traditional and nontraditional tools can be used for that task:
rewards, a climate of innovation, hiring innovative people, encouraging the cross-pollination of ideas, and providing support for innovators. Management's responsibilities in the area of innovation are
treated extensively in chapter 14, nevertheless, let's consider here
some of the things that management can do to encourage the idea
generation part of the process.

Rewards

Reward idea generators with pay and/or promotions. Rewards provide a clear signal that good ideas are important. Monetary rewards appear to be more effective when they are performance-based and when they give employees a personal stake in organizational success. Many innovative companies, 3M being one example, use dual career ladders—technical and managerial—to reward innovative behavior. They realize that not everyone is cut out to be a manager, nor wishes to be one.

Rewards for innovators, however, should encompass more than pay and promotions. Pay and promotion prevent feelings of being taken advantage of, but they do not drive the free thinking needed for innovation. For many people, the rewards that lead to innovation involve greater freedom: to explore hunches, to pursue one's curiosity, to travel to technical conferences, to mingle with customers and lead users, and so forth. Access to greater resources is also an effective reward when innovation is the goal.

A Climate of Innovation

Management determines the organizational climate. Innovative organizations have these characteristics:

- Management sends a clear message that the well-being of the company and its employees depends on continuous innovation.

- People aren't afraid to try or suggest new things.

- No one feels a sense of entitlement for just showing up for work.

- There is a visceral discomfort with current success—a nagging sense that it may not last.

- People rise and fall on their merits and contributions.

- Employees are outward looking; they seek ideas and best practices among competitors, through professional contacts, and within other industries.

If the climate of your company lacks these characteristics, change it.

Hire Innovative People

Some people are better at generating ideas than others. Ed Roberts and Alan Fusfeld identified the personal characteristics of idea generators; these individuals:

- Are experts in one or two fields

- Enjoy doing innovative work

- Are usually individual contributors

- Are good problem solvers

- Find new and different ways of seeing things[16]

Many of these characteristics can be identified in the normal hiring process: in résumés, hiring interviews, and reference checks. So be on the lookout for them. Look in particular for these individuals:

- Engineers with broad interests who can bridge the boundaries between technical disciplines

- Technical people who nevertheless like to meet customers and wrestle with their problems

- Continual learners

As a general rule it's wise to avoid hiring hyperspecialists—people who want to learn more and more about less and less. Also, avoid hiring anyone who has no interest in customers or their problems.

Management can also encourage ideas by *avoiding* policies and practices that make creativity unlikely. For example, if people are operating under a dark cloud of fear, drive out that fear. Some managers create fear by punishing failure, which only encourages people to play it safe and take no risks. Robert I. Sutton suggests something different: he recommends that managers reward success and failure, but punish *inaction*.[17] He cites the advice of IBM's legendary founder,

Thomas Watson, who told people, "If you want to succeed, double your failure rate." Thus, every failure brings you closer to success; inaction will get you nowhere.

If there is a "suits versus lab coats" mentality in the workplace, management should spend more one-on-one time with the lab coats. If people are being driven to 120 percent of capacity, lighten up; create space for musing.

Encourage the Cross-Pollination of Ideas

Ideas and knowledge often produce little when they are isolated in organizational pockets, but something magical happens when they are allowed to float free. Formerly isolated ideas come together to produce something new. You can encourage this cross-pollination of ideas by any of the following means:

- Periodically reassign technical specialists to different work teams. The resulting interactions often lead to insights, or the novel application of one technology to another.

- Send people to professional conferences and scientific convocations.

- Set up an *intra*company knowledge management system—this makes knowledge and experience captured in one area available to everyone.

- Sponsor events that bring outside experts to your company to give lectures and workshops—what they have to share often catalyzes ideas within the company.

- Arrange periodic customer site visits and field trips to observe best practices in other industries.

- Meet with local inventors and entrepreneurs in your field.

- Seek out consultants with different perspectives.

- Invite university professors on sabbatical to temporarily join your group or participate in brainstorming sessions.

Each of these approaches takes advantage of the power of networking. 3M, which has maintained a high level of innovation for over one hundred years, views formal and informal networking among its scientists as one of its secret weapons. In 1951 it institutionalized the formal part of its network with the creation of the Technical Forum. The Forum hosts an annual symposium to which all of the company's R&D personnel are invited and given an opportunity to learn what their colleagues in other technical fields are working on (the company supports more than forty-two technical fields) and to build personal relationships and better communication between scientists. That sort of communication and knowledge sharing has resulted in researchers taking an idea from one realm and applying it to another. For example, 3M scientists have used a technology initially developed for layered plastic lenses to create more durable abrasives.

Support Innovators

Just as artists have always needed the help of wealthy patrons to pursue their muses, innovators need the support of highly placed managers. Without that support, many ideas die on the vine.

Management support need not—and often should not—take the form of formal funding and staff resources, particularly in the early stages. But senior managers can provide the resources that innovators need to "bootleg" unofficial development of their ideas:

- Unused space in which to conduct experiments

- Small sums for equipment and part-time help

- Time away from regular duties in which to pursue an idea

Senior managers can also protect worthy ideas from the organizational mechanisms that kill off ideas. What are these mechanisms?

- **A negative view of ideas that don't serve existing customers:**
  This is the "tyranny of served market" syndrome again. *Antidote:* Remind people that current customers are just a segment of the customer universe. The new idea may be just the ticket

for another segment. Also remember that current customers who don't like the new idea may change their tune once the idea is perfected and competitively priced.

- **The new idea threatens the current business:** "If we did this we'd simply cannibalize our existing sales." *Antidote:* Remember that if you don't eat up your current business with different (i.e., superior) products, someone else will. Wouldn't you rather keep that revenue than give it away?

- **The market potential seems too small relative to the size of the existing business:** Big companies miss out on many important innovations because the potential is viewed—often erroneously—as too small. "We're a $2 billion company. Why would we mess around with something that might only contribute $5 million to sales?" This is a powerful argument, since companies need to maintain focus. *Antidote:* Remember that many innovations initially appeal to small niches, but expand as the technology improves and customers find new and unanticipated uses for them. For example, initial market research on a new-fangled machine called the "computer" indicated world demand for only ten machines; the only imagined customers were national defense and scientific organizations. Likewise, the Internet was initially conceived of as a communications link for the academic/scientific community.

Four Idea-Generating Techniques

Companies use a variety of techniques to generate new ideas. Four are offered here: brainstorming, nominal group technique, TRIZ, and catchball.

Brainstorming

Most readers have had some experience with brainstorming, a method of soliciting ideas from a group of individuals in rapid fashion that does not examine ideas as they emerge Effective brainstorming is guided by five key principles:

1. **Focus:** Brainstorming should concentrate on a particular problem or opportunity and be bounded by real-world constraints.

2. **Suspended judgment:** All judging should be suspended while ideas are being generated. Even the wildest ideas should be encouraged.

3. **Personal safety:** Participates should be assured that unpopular ideas or ideas that threaten the status quo will not provoke recriminations.

4. **Serial discussion:** Limit the discussion to one conversation at a time and keep it focused on the topic.

5. **Build on ideas:** Try to build on the ideas of others wherever possible.

Brainstorming techniques fall into several broad categories: visioning, modifying, and experimenting. Each category uses a slightly different thought process, but there are some common features. Modifying and experimenting techniques, for example, start with existing data and use intuitive insights to draw ideas from those facts. Vision techniques use the intuitive process first, and then follow up with information gathering and data analysis.

VISIONING. This approach asks people to imagine, in detail, a long-term, ideal solution and the means of achieving it—for example, a home heating system based on alternative technologies (see worksheet 2-1 for a template for this exercise). The goal is to break free of the ingrained practicality that inhibits innovative thought. Once you've generated several ideas that would constitute that ideal solution, participants can then discuss what it would take to make those ideas happen.

Visioning techniques worksheet

These techniques help participants imagine the future, usually the ideal future.

Wish list

Generating wishes

Ask people to "let themselves go" and imagine an ideal situation in which, for example, they would be granted any wish they want by a fairy godmother, by winning the lottery and having unlimited resources, or by whatever else sets the tone. Select a quiet place without interruptions, or play soothing background music.

Exploring the possibilities

Encourage everyone to review their lists: what did they discover about themselves or the situation? Then take it another step: what would it actually take to make this wish come true?

The ideal scenario

Ask the group to imagine what the ideal future or solution would look like. This can be done with words or with images. For example, participants could pour through visually rich magazines, select images and paste them together in a collage. Follow the creation with discussion and exploration.

Time machine

Alternatively, ask participants to pretend that they can time travel to 5–7 years into the future. What would the situation look like then? What would have been accomplished? Add whatever questions are relevant to the creative challenge being explored.

SOURCE: Harvard ManageMentor® on Innovation © 2000 by the President and Fellows of Harvard College and its licensors. All rights reserved. Inspired by tools in William C. Miller, *Flash of Brilliance* (Reading, MA: Perseus Books, 1999).

MODIFYING. Visioning techniques begin by assuming that there are no constraints. Modifying techniques, on the other hand, begin with the status quo—with current technology or conditions—and try to make adaptations. One good way to see how your current product or service could be modified is to look at it from the customer's perspective. Consider every feature of the product or service and how that feature adds or diminishes value for you.

EXPERIMENTING. Experimenting helps people to systematically combine elements in various ways and then test the combinations. One such approach involves creating a matrix. For example, a car-wash owner in search of a new market or market extension would begin by listing parameters across the top: method, products washed, equipment, and products sold; under each parameter, he lists all the possible variations he can think of. Under the equipment category, the variations might include sprays, conveyors, stalls, dryers, and brushes; the products washed category might include cars, houses, clothes, and dogs. The resulting table allows the owner to put together new business possibilities using alternatives listed under the columns. Thus, he might decide to start a service for boat owners to wash their boats using the existing stalls and brushes.

Nominal Group Technique

Brainstorming is a proven and popular technique for drawing ideas out of individuals and getting people to talk about those ideas. Its informality makes it easy to apply. However, the method depends on people speaking up and contributing in a group setting. Unfortunately, many brainstorming participants, for one reason or another, will not speak up. Some fear appearing stupid. Others lack confidence in their ideas or want to withhold those ideas until they've developed them to a higher level. Still others remain silent when their ideas are in opposition to those advocated by more powerful members of the group or by the group's consensus. Whatever the reason, the group setting of brainstorming has a way of silencing some people.

A remedy for this problem is *nominal group technique* (NGT). Like brainstorming, NGT aims to evoke ideas and problem solutions from participants. But NGT is designed to evoke participation from *all* members of the group. Here's how it works. Twelve or fewer people are seated around a table, with one acting as facilitator and another as recorder. Unlike brainstorming, participants are not asked to orally contribute; instead, they are told to *write down* their ideas and give them, anonymously, to the recorder. Thus, all participants, including people who may be reluctant to speak up in front of a group, share their ideas.

Once the recorder has collected all the ideas in written form, the facilitator reads them to the entire group. Participants are asked to rate each idea in order of perceived value, using a 0 to 10 scale. These ratings are returned anonymously to the recorder, who totals each idea's ratings and posts them for all to see. Participants then discuss the ideas in a normal way. They know how the group rated each idea, but still have no clue about who offered them or who gave a high or low rating.

NGT has two benefits relative to brainstorming:

1. A few big talkers or politically powerful people are less likely to dominate the idea pool and the discussion.

2. NGT achieves participation from everyone, including those who might not offer ideas to a large group.

TRIZ

One weakness of both brainstorming and NGT is their randomness. Whether the thoughts flying out from the minds of participants contain anything useful or connect with other thoughts in ways that spark useful insight is not controllable or predictable. This weakness has encouraged some to embrace a *theory of inventive problem solving*, or *TRIZ*. TRIZ was developed in Russia by scientist Genrich Altshuller and his colleagues over several decades, beginning in the late 1940s. This method systematically solves problems and creates innovation by identifying and eliminating what Altshuller called technical contradictions.[18]

One popular example of the TRIZ method is the development of the incandescent lamp by Thomas Edison in the late 1800s. Earlier tinkerers knew that they could create light by passing electricity through a conductive medium, such as a metal wire filament. The contradiction, in this case, was the fact that the wire would quickly burn up. Edison eventually resolved this contradiction by placing his wire within a vacuum tube and finding filament material with a practical working life (in this case, carbonized thread).

Undocumented reports state that sixty thousand engineers around the world are trained in TRIZ methods, and enthusiasts cite its use by many big-name industrial companies as evidence of its effectiveness.

Catchball

Among their other contributions to management methods, the Japanese have given us *catchball*. Catchball is a cross-functional method for accomplishing two goals: idea enrichment/improvement, and buy-in among participants.[19] Once you've generated an idea, you can build and improve on it using this method.

Here's how it works. An initial idea is "tossed" to collaborators for consideration, as in figure 2-1. The idea may be a new strategic goal, a new product, or a way to improve some work process. Whoever "catches" the idea assumes responsibility for understanding it and improving it in some way. That person then tosses the improved idea back to the group, where it is again caught and improved still further. And around it goes in a cycle of gradual improvement. As people participate, they develop a sense of shared ownership and commitment to the idea that takes form.

Catchball's underlying principle goes back to the Socratic method of dialogue first articulated by Plato. Try using it the next time your organization needs to develop a raw idea and get people committed to it.

FIGURE 2-1

Catchball

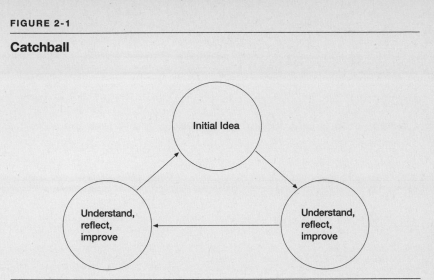

Summing Up

Ideas are the nutrients of innovation. You can't get anywhere without them. And in the innovation race, organizations with many good ideas to pick from have a real advantage. This chapter has examined key sources of innovative ideas:

- **New knowledge:** Though the trail from new knowledge to marketable products is often long, this is the source of many, if not most, radical innovations.

- **Customers' ideas:** These ideas can tell you where current products fall short and point to unmet needs.

- **Lead users:** These are people (or companies) whose needs are far ahead of market trends. Look at what they're doing today to meet needs that others many discover tomorrow.

- **Empathetic design:** This is an idea-generating technique whereby innovators observe how people use existing products and services in their own environments. So try going out and

observing how customers and potential customers do things
and attempt to solve problems.

- **Invention factories and skunkworks:** These are R&D labs and
  special projects with singular missions and their own quarters.

- **Open market innovation:** Open market innovation relies on
  the free trading of ideas between entities through licensing,
  joint ventures, and strategic alliances.

- **Idea-generating techniques:** Such techniques include brainstorming, nominal group technique, TRIZ, and catchball.

3

Recognizing Opportunities

Innovator as Entrepreneur

Key Topics Covered in This Chapter

- *A method for recognizing value*

- *Rough cut business evaluation of opportunities*

- *Tips for enhancing opportunity recognition*

CHAPTER 2 DESCRIBED the many sources of innovative ideas and what management can do to generate them. Ideas are fuel for the innovation process. By themselves, however, they benefit no one. Someone must see in a particular idea its potential for creating value—opportunity recognition. There's a big difference between an interesting idea and an idea that represents real business or societal value. Can you tell the difference?

Opportunity recognition has been defined by Mark Rice and Gina Colarelli O'Connor as "the match between an unfulfilled market need and a solution that satisfied the need."[1] Recognition triggers the evaluation that moves an idea down the long and often bumpy road toward commercialization. It is a mental process that answers a question every innovator must ask: Does this idea represent real value to anyone? Being able to answer this question correctly is probably as important as having an innovative idea or developing a scientific breakthrough. Some have articulated opportunity recognition in memorable ways. As Thomas Edison told a newspaper reporter after witnessing a demonstration of electric arc lighting, "I have struck a big bonanza."

The opportunities of most innovations are not always obvious. 3M scientist Art Fry had an idea for which he foresaw a very limited opportunity: using a weak adhesive to make notepaper stick to other things—specifically, as place markers for his church choir's hymnals. The larger business opportunity for his idea took time to emerge as Post-it notes.

"What can we do with this?" is a question that idea generators must answer; and in some cases the answers are slow in coming, especially when the innovative idea is radical—new to the world and not simply an incremental advance on an existing concept. The technological and market uncertainties that go hand in hand with radical ideas make it difficult for people to see the potential opportunities they contain. DuPont's developers of Biomax, a biodegradable polymer material, took several years to answer the question. Initially, DuPont researchers thought that thin sheets of their interesting new material could be used as liners for disposable baby diapers. But the diaper manufacturers weren't interested. After putting the material on the shelf for a long period, someone thought of using it in the banana groves of Central America, where its ability to protect fruit until it reached harvesting age and then disintegrate into a harmless mulch would be a real benefit. But that didn't prove to be much of a business either. But since then, many applications have been found for this interesting and versatile material.[2]

Even when an opportunity is recognized, it may be small relative to the innovation's full potential. This is what happened to the radio early in the twentieth century. Inventor Guiseppe Marconi made great strides in wireless telegraphy, as he called it, in the 1890s. The opportunity he recognized for this development was important but limited: ship-to-shore communication. Governments, shippers, and marine insurers were interested, enough so that Marconi could launch a successful business. And his innovation is credited with saving thousands of lives at sea—seven hundred from the 1912 sinking of the *Titanic* alone. But the true commercial potential of radio-wave transmission eluded Marconi until 1922, when the first wireless transmission of musical entertainment was made. Suddenly, radio was more than a means of sending Morse coded messages between stations. Its potential as a broadcast medium for sharing news and entertainment with the masses was finally recognized.

Marconi's narrowly conceived opportunity for radio technology is not unique. The Internet, which was initially viewed as a rapid communications medium for the scientific community, followed a similar trajectory. Its utility for the broader public and for business-to-consumer and business-to-business commerce were recognized only later. In this sense, opportunity recognition is often an unfolding process. The initial window of opportunity is a passageway to others.

As Rice and O'Connor have pointed out through a number of examples, opportunity recognition may be necessary at more than one stage of the innovation process. They cite the case of GE's development of digital X-ray technology, where many instances of opportunity recognition were identified, each at a different phase in the technology's long journey toward eventual commercialization: "the research scientist (1984); someone from the outside firm (1987); the first head of the business unit (1988); the head of central research (1992); the CEO (1993); and the second head of the business unit (1997)."[3] The merits of the project had to be recognized at each point in order to maintain support and funding, and also because the nature of the opportunity itself was not fixed.

A Method for Opportunity Recognition

Recognizing the opportunity associated with an innovation is usually chancy. Data about the innovation's performance in use is either limited or speculative. How customers will respond to a commercial version of the innovation can only be inferred. As a result, many innovators either fail to recognize opportunities or overestimate them.

Although there is no proven formula for opportunity recognition, W. Chan Kim and Renée Mauborgne described a method called the buyer utility map that indicates the likelihood that customers will be attracted to a new idea or product.[4] Kim and Mauborgne believe in focusing on an innovation's utility—how it will change the lives or work of customers. The buyer utility map, shown in figure 3-1, helps innovators to think about two things: (1) the levers they can pull in delivering utility to customers, and (2) the various stages in

FIGURE 3-1

The buyer utility map

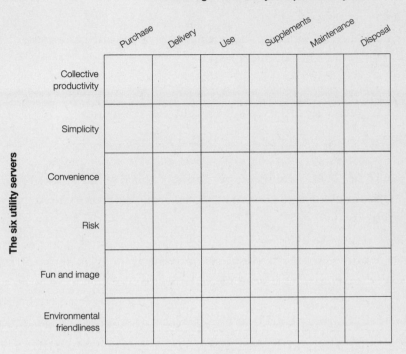

The six stages of the buyer experience cycle

Source: W. Chan Kim and Reneé Mauborgne, "Knowing a Winning Idea When You See One," *Harvard Business Review*, September–October 2000, 129–138.

the "buyer experience cycle," a cycle that runs from purchase through disposal. Each stage encompasses a wide variety of specific experiences. An innovator can use this map to identify the utility offered by the new product or service at various stages of the buyer experience cycle.

Kim and Mauborgne offer the example of discount broker Charles Schwab. With 24/7 phone (and later online) service, Schwab created utility in the "convenience-purchase" cell of the matrix. By offering instantaneous trade confirmations over a secure connection it also offered utility in the "risk-purchase" cell.

You can use this utility-buyer experience map to assess the utility an innovative idea. Ask yourself:

- Where can we create the greatest utility for our customers? Does our idea fill this space?

- Is that utility higher or lower than the utility created by existing products or services offered by our competitors?

- Which of these utilities matters most to customers?

- How could we redesign our product/service idea to offer the greatest utility to customers in the areas that matter most to them?

In answering each question, you can get a good sense of the business potential of an innovative idea.

Another approach is *perceptual mapping*, a market research tool used to compare products or product ideas against the perceptions of customers. A perceptual map is (usually) a two-dimensional space on which alternative product or product ideas are plotted against their attributes or the primary needs of customers. Decision makers then have a graphic image of the "positioning" of their product ideas relative to primary customer needs. For example, figure 3-2 is a perceptual map created for men's wrist watches. It indicates roughly how customers perceive many of leading brands in terms of two dimensions: sporty versus fashion, and upscale/precision versus affordable. Notice that these dimensions create market segments.

For innovators, and for decision makers who must evaluate their ideas, a perceptual map can be used to locate unserved segments. In figure 3-2, for example, if Casio didn't exist, the innovator and management would be able to identify an unserved segment in the sporty-affordable quadrant. They would then know how better to direct scarce idea-development resources.

FIGURE 3-2

Perception mapping—men's watches

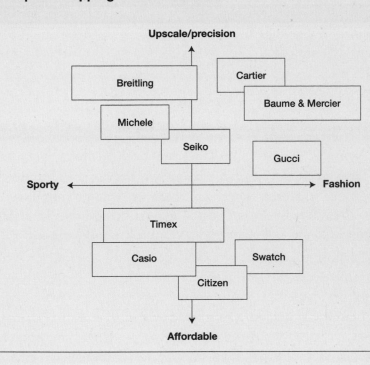

Rough Cut Business Evaluation

Let's assume that your innovative idea qualifies as a legitimate opportunity—that is, it has real value for customers. One more task is required before the idea can move forward into development and formal market research: a rough cut business evaluation. A rough cut business evaluation considers three fundamental questions:

1. Does the innovation have a strategic fit with your company?

2. Do you have the technical competencies to make it work?

3. Do you have the business competencies to make it successful?

Note that a rough cut evaluation is qualitative. More complete and quantitative idea screening comes later, as the idea becomes more completely formed. At this point, you simply want to determine if some individual or team should use time and resources to investigate the idea and develop it further. The end point for this type of evaluation should be a formal business plan (see appendix A for a sample business plan).

Strategic Fit

You may have a great idea, but if that idea lacks strategic fit with your company, its development and commercialization could create long-term problems. For example, a new system for making espresso coffee in half the time would not have a strategic fit with discount broker Charles Schwab, but a new and easy-to-use financial planning software program would. That's obvious, but the strategic fit of ideas floating around your company are bound to be much less obvious, so be very thoughtful as you think through the question of strategic fit.

What should you do with a good idea that lacks strategic fit? A good idea, almost by definition, has profit potential—for someone. But in ill-equipped hands, that potential may never be realized. Also, pushing into unfamiliar terrain with an innovation is risky. Thus, the choices are threefold: either drop the idea, license it to someone who can do something with it, or create a separate or joint venture organization to develop it. Let's consider the last two.

The motives behind licensing agreements are widely observed. Here's a classic example. A small pharmaceutical company develops and gains regulatory approval to produce and sell a new drug. But it has neither manufacturing capabilities nor effective distribution networks. It determines that its best option is to license manufacturing and distribution to a major pharmaceutical company in return for an upfront payment and a royalty on sales. Thus the innovator captures value from its invention even though it lacks the capacity to make it commercially successful.

The joint venture operates on the same principle, bringing together complementary resources to capture value. Here, the innovator teams up with an organization that possesses the missing

Tips for Enhancing Opportunity Recognition

Though opportunity recognition takes place in the minds of individual employees, management can take steps to facilitate it. It can:

- **Be very clear about company strategy and long-term objectives:** This helps people answer the question, "Does my idea fit with company strategy?" That question cannot be answered if people don't understand the strategy.

- **Expose research scientists and engineers to customers and marketing:** This exposure arms the opportunity recognition mechanism within these individuals.

- **Give people with ideas a place to take them:** In their study of radical innovation, Richard Leifer and his colleagues note that the technical professionals who generate so many breakthrough ideas don't always have the breadth of experience to recognize the opportunities they represent. They need a place to take their idea—a place where they can ask the question: "What could we do with this?" That "place" is often a business development manager who serves as a link between the company's R&D efforts and the world of customers and their problems.[a]

a. Richard Leifer et al., *Radical Innovation: How Mature Companies Can Outsmart Upstarts* (Boston: Harvard Business School Press, 2000), 142–155.

resources, capabilities, or market access. Working together, the two (or more) organizations have a chance of making a success of the recognized opportunity.

Technical Competencies

Every company has one or more technical competencies. A securities broker-dealer has competencies in trading, market making, and information systems. A mini-mill steel company has technical competencies in metallurgy, manufacturing, and logistics, among others. Does your company have the technical know-how to successfully develop a particular idea? If it does not, could that know-how be acquired?

Business Competencies

Business competencies include marketing, distribution, new-product development, the ability to serve a particular customer base, the ability to manage widely scattered employees and facilities, and so forth. What are your core business competencies? Are they the same ones your innovative idea will need in order to become successful? If your company lacks any of the required competencies, ask yourself if the idea is big enough to justify the effort and expense of developing those competencies.

Summing Up

This chapter has explored the important activity of opportunity recognition, which attempts to answer a fundamental question: Does this idea represent real value to current or potential customers? To help you be successful in this activity, this chapter has considered the following:

- **A method for recognizing value:** This method is based on Kim and Mauborgne's buyer utility map, which helps innovators to think about two things: (1) the levers they can pull in delivering utility to customers, and (2) the various stages in the buyer experience cycle, which runs from purchase to disposal.

- **Perceptual mapping:** Perceptual mapping is a market research tool used to compare products or product ideas against the perceptions of customers. A perceptual map is (usually) a two-dimensional space on which alternative product or product ideas are plotted against their attributes or the primary needs of customers.

- **Rough cut business evaluation:** This evaluation of opportunities offers another nonquantitative screen that separates good ideas from the rest. It asks three fundamental questions: Does the innovation have a strategic fit with the company? Does the company have the technical competencies to make it work? Does the company have the business competencies to make it successful? If you get positive answers to all three, the idea has potential.

- **Tips for enhancing opportunity recognition.**

Finally, the chapter suggests several things that management can do to facilitate opportunity recognition among employees.

4

From Recognition to Support

Gaining a Foothold

Key Topics Covered in This Chapter

- *The critical role of the idea champion and other supporters in gaining broader recognition and support*

- *The importance of timing in gaining recognition and support*

- *How to build a business case for the innovative idea*

- *Overcoming resistance and maintaining momentum*

"NE SCIENTIST HAD *been running around evan-gelizing the technology for two or three years. He hadn't been able to build a case that got it recognized and funded. What we had here was a corporate research fellow, one of the smartest guys in the world, but he couldn't get the attention to tilt this thing up.*"[1]

That's how an IBM business development manager described the problem faced by one of his company's innovators, as reported by Richard Leifer and his fellow investigators of radical innovation in large companies. Recognizing an idea's potential is an important step in the innovation process. But getting the "right" people to recognize the idea—that is, people with the power to allocate resources—is another hurdle, and one that demands substantial organizational skill and entrepreneurial drive. Many people have ideas—some excellent. But few demonstrate the savvy and tenacity needed to turn their ideas into realities. Those that do are true entrepreneurs.

This chapter identifies practical steps the entrepreneur/innovator can take to move beyond initial recognition to a situation involving greater support. These require that someone act as the idea's champion, and that others act in facilitative roles. Movement toward wider recognition and support also involves building a business case and, in some instances, overcoming resistance.

The Champion

The *champion* assumes responsibility for moving a promising innovative idea (or project) toward the market. The champion need not be the idea's creator, but must have the enthusiasm and commitment needed to promote and implement it. He or she will need both in good measure, as frustration and setbacks are bound to be encountered along on the road to success.

Research suggests that a committed champion is critical to the successful implementation of an idea, especially if the idea represents a radical innovation opportunity or if the need for it is not widely recognized. A powerful idea can remain dormant in a company for years if no one assumes responsibility for advancing it. In the hands of a person with technical know-how, energy, daring, dedication, and perseverance, however, the same idea can advance.

Supporting Cast

The effort of a single champion working alone is rarely sufficient to take an idea from concept to broad-based recognition to full development. Typically, no single person controls all of the information, expertise, and resources required to bring an idea to fruition. Implementing an innovative idea requires the support and assistance of many people in the champion's network of superiors, peers, mentors, or colleagues. Among these are sponsors, gatekeepers, opinion leaders, and influencers.

Sponsors

A *sponsor* is usually a senior person who holds a position of power and who controls some level of resources (see "A Sponsor Can Save the Day"). This person often provides help with implementation problems and suggests ways in which the champion can present an idea most effectively to management. The sponsor frequently works

A Sponsor Can Save the Day

In their book *Radical Innovation*, Richard Leifer and his colleagues made an important observation about each of the ten cases they studied.[a] In each instance a highly placed sponsor, or patron, was instrumental in providing critical services. These sponsors kept their projects alive by providing funding—sometimes through normal channels, sometimes under the table. They deflected attempts to terminate innovative projects and promoted the value of project objectives to higher management. Without the protection and support of these patrons, each of the ten projects studied would have died or limped along, starved for funds.

Innovators should be careful about whom they approach to play the sponsor's role. The sponsor should have organizational clout and, ideally, some "skin in the game." A sponsor who has nothing to lose if the idea gets squashed (or nothing to gain if it succeeds) is of questionable value as a sponsor.

a. Richard Leifer et al., *Radical Innovation: How Mature Companies Can Outsmart Upstarts* (Boston: Harvard Business School Press, 2000), 163.

behind the scenes to supply resources and to protect the idea from premature extermination from naysayers and internal competitors for resources. Once he had achieved fame, Thomas Edison could claim Cornelius Vanderbilt and J. P. Morgan as sponsors. Hyman Rickover played this role for the nuclear U.S. Navy. Corning innovators of fiber optics could look to Tom Macavoy for support over many years; and Geoff Nicholson nursed along the team that developed Post-it notes for 3M.

Gatekeepers

Another important role is filled by so-called *gatekeepers*. Gatekeepers are usually experts in functional areas such as R&D, manufacturing, or sales. They are up-to-date in their function specific area of knowledge and can serve as useful sounding boards and information resources as the champion develops the idea and builds a business case for it. Because of their contact networks, gatekeepers can connect the project with people who can provide additional information, expertise, or other resources.

Opinion Leaders and Influencers

One of the champion's primary challenges is to influence decision makers to recognize and support the innovative idea. One way to do that is to approach decision makers directly. Another is to approach them indirectly through opinion leaders and influencers in the organization. *Opinion leaders* are respected for their expertise, judgment, and insights. These are the "go-to" people to whom others turn when seeking information or making decisions. The opinion leader's endorsement of an idea lends credibility and helps accelerate its acceptance. On the other hand, an opinion leader who does not like an idea can cause its support to evaporate. Thus, the champion must exercise care when sharing ideas with opinion leaders. Sharing them prematurely, before they have reached a credible point of development, could result in their demise.

Influencers, like opinion leaders, are individuals who participate indirectly in the decision-making process. They provide advice and information to key stakeholders and decision makers. For example, if you're trying to persuade a marketing manager to launch a new Web campaign, she may turn to the head of information technology for advice on the matter. In this sense, the IT person has influence over the decision.

Harvard professor Michael Watkins refers to influence networks and suggests that anyone aiming to persuade others should map out these networks to better understand the complex relationships of influence between members of the organization.[2] Figure 4-1 is an influence map involving four people. The degree of influence between individuals is represented there by the thickness of the arrows that

FIGURE 4-1

Influence map

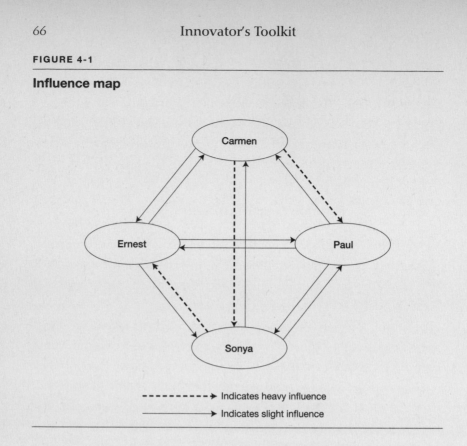

connect them. Thus, Carmen has substantial influence over both Paul and Sonya, but these individuals, as indicated by the narrow thickness of their arrows, have less influence over Carmen.

Whether you sketch it out on paper or in your head, an influence map can help you understand where to apply persuasion in a group setting. Again, using figure 4–1 as an example, if you were trying to persuade Ernest about some matter, you would apply indirect influence through Sonya, and possibly through Carmen because she has influence over Sonya.

Get the Timing Right

Typically, successful innovators build a supportive network of peers, colleagues, and sponsors *before* seeking support at higher levels. Timing one's approach of upper-level executives can be tricky. For example, periods of senior-level leadership flux or financial crisis are seldom the best times to spring new ideas on top managers, who are probably too distracted to give them adequate attention. On the other hand, waiting too long to approach upper management can be as problematic as approaching them too early. Some key decision makers should be brought on board relatively quickly; doing so will give the champion and other supporters some assurance that they have formal support and that resources are likely to follow. Many people will not support the champion without that assurance.

Timing is an area in which the sponsor's political savvy and knowledge of how the company operates can make a unique contribution. The sponsor can help the champion to develop a strategy for approaching top management and stakeholders at the appropriate time.

Build a Business Case

Once a champion has assembled a support network and identified stakeholders, it's time to build a business case for the innovative idea. A *business case* brings together the information needed to demonstrate the merits of an innovative idea to management and other stakeholders. Building a business case involves both creative thinking about how the innovation could unfold and analytical thinking about how the idea will impact the organization and its employees, customers, and other stakeholders. The thinking and debate that go into the creation of the business case are as important as the final document itself.

A typical business case contains the following key sections:

- **Goals:** Describe the idea and what it aims to achieve.

- **Describe the business model:** How will this idea produce money? By collecting fees for services? By selling Web site ads? By allowing the company to profitably sell its products at a much lower cost than competitors?

- **Benefits:** How will the idea benefit customers or end-users as well as your company? Explain why the idea is an improvement over the status quo and the potential competitive advantage it could give your company. Will it produce measurable improvements in costs, revenues, profit, or customer satisfaction?

- **Fit:** Explain why this idea is a good fit for your company in terms of how it complements existing technology, strategic plans, manufacturing capabilities, and/or plans for future expansion. The job of gaining management support will be much more difficult if the innovative idea is not related to the company's current line of business, product lines, or strategic direction.

- **Milestones:** List the major milestones you propose for the idea's implementation (prototype development, market test, ramp-up, and so forth). Do this without getting bogged down in the details of each step you'll take. Management is usually reluctant to support an "open-ended" concept that has no time constraints.

- **Potential obstacles:** Acknowledge potential problems or risks to show that you have considered them. Examples of potential problems and risks include technical issues that may or may not be overcome, the need to educate customers about the merits and uses of the innovation, and so forth. As part of the business case, provide a plan for addressing these potential obstacles.

- **Cost estimate for implementing the innovation:** Include specific numbers wherever possible.

- **Resource requirements:** Indicate the resources—people, skills, equipment, budget, etc.—needed to reach key milestones.

To complement the business case, the champion should craft an "elevator speech" that describes the innovation and its benefits to customers and the company. This capsule presentation can be used to get someone interested in your idea when you have access to that person. An effective elevator speech is:

- **Short:** No more than four or five sentences. If you need fifteen or twenty minutes to explain the idea and its benefits, you won't be able to sell it to others.

- **Clear:** The listener shouldn't have to say, "I don't get it—could you explain that?" People will not support ideas that confuse them.

- **Compelling:** You want the listener to think, "Wow! That sounds important." If your elevator speech is compelling, the listener will give you an opportunity to describe the idea in greater detail ("I like your idea and I'd like to learn more about it. Let's talk about it over lunch on Thursday. I'll bring along the CFO").

Refine your business case and elevator speech as you gather new information or gain insight into how to get people excited about your project. Then go a step further—develop a full-blown business plan using the information in appendix A as a model.

Line Up Stakeholders

Success in gaining recognition and support for an innovative idea depends greatly on the champion's ability to gain the adherence of key stakeholders. Before even building a business case, stakeholders and their interests regarding the innovative idea should be identified. Then, using their interests and the idea's potential benefits for them, the champion can prepare a strategy for gaining their support. That strategy should address the things that matter most to the individual stakeholders and how they prefer to receive information and influence. (The strategy should also take into account likely resisters; see "Deal with Resistance.") To gain the support of the vice president of finance, for example, the champion would likely

Deal with Resistance

Many innovations challenge the status quo. Those that do may encounter resistance. For example, a product line manager may feel threatened by an idea for of a new, better product if it would render his product line obsolete or cannibalize its sales. Savvy innovation champions and idea sponsors anticipate this type of resistance and find ways to diffuse it, work around it, or, if given no other choice, roll over it.

Resistance to new ideas is often a symptom of one or more underlying issues:

• Fear of the unknown

• A belief that the innovation is unnecessary or of little value

• A personality conflict with the idea's creator and/or its adherents

• The desire to protect oneself from risk or uncertainty

• A difference in outlooks

• Lack of reward or personal benefits for accepting change

• Concern that implementation of the innovation will increase the workload or compete for limited resources

Identifying the cause of the resistance is the first step in over-coming it.

How do you move a resister to your point of view? The key lies in understanding the resister's position and then presenting the benefits of your idea in terms the resister values. The following guidelines can help.

Identify Resisters' Interests

If you encounter resistance after presenting an idea or proposal, avoid the temptation to keep pressing your case. Instead, think about what may be driving a resister to disagree with you. Adapt your response accordingly. For example, suppose you are seeking funding to experiment with a new distribution concept for your company. Another manager opposes your plan. She is concerned that it will channel company resources away from a project she wants to pursue. In her mind, the two of you are in a zero-sum game in which any gain by you will be a loss for her. In this case, you might want to address her fears by demonstrating, if you can, that it's not a zero-sum game. You might argue that the success of your idea will generate additional revenues for the company, which in turn will make more funds available for her projects.

Build Trust

Another way to reduce resistance is to build trust. You can do that by listening carefully to resisters' concerns. By listening, you demonstrate that you understand and value them as individuals and care about their ideas and concerns. When people feel that they've been heard and that their ideas are valued, they will become more open to your ideas.

Incorporate Elements of the Resister's Idea

In many cases, a good idea can be strengthened by incorporating elements of someone else's idea—creating a hybrid that is superior to either of the two original ideas. Can you think of an example from your own experience? Incorporating some part of a resister's idea into your own may improve your concept even as its turns the resister into a collaborator.

prepare a formal presentation with extensive printed supporting materials such as cost estimates, industry spending trends, and the competitive advantage implicit in the innovation. The finance professional is interested in the funding level to develop the idea, future cash flow streams, return on investment, and how long the company will have to wait to realize a positive return. The champion must address those interests. The vice president of marketing, another important stakeholder, will likely have other concerns and prefer a different style for receiving information. For her, the "customer benefits" of the innovative idea may matter most. And unlike the finance person, she may have a preference for verbal and conceptual, versus written, information.

Maintain Momentum

Innovative ideas take time to bear fruit, often because they periodically lose momentum and languish for one reason or another: the champion is transferred and a new one must be found; the well of financial support has temporarily run dry; the idea is shifted from one business unit to another for development; the initial market opportunity has not panned out and a new one must be found; and so forth.

Maintaining momentum for an innovative idea or project is difficult. It is much easier to get people excited over a vision at the beginning of a project than it is to maintain their enthusiasm during months or years of project work. Success in maintaining momentum often depends on the champion's undiminished enthusiasm and persistence. Here are a few tips for maintaining momentum:

- Keep up a regular stream of communication with the sponsor, supporters, stakeholders, top management, and opinion leaders.

- Make key stakeholders and managers ad hoc members of the innovation team. Invite them to working lunches where progress and obstacles are discussed.

- Demonstrate early prototypes to key people.

Momentum is important because the path from idea recognition to implementation of the idea may be long and challenging, the subject of chapter 5.

Summing Up

A great idea alone is insufficient for success. The innovator must gain acceptance for it from individuals and organizations that have the resources to further its development and eventual commercialization. Gaining acceptance usually involves:

- A *champion* assuming responsibility for the idea who embodies the energy, enthusiasm, and conviction needed to overcome resistance and gain support

- A supporting cast of advocates, including a sponsor with political/organizational clout, gatekeepers, opinion leaders, and influencers

- Proper timing of the campaign to convince management of the innovation's merits

- A business case that will convince management and give it the information it needs to make a good decision

- Support from a range of stakeholders

- Strategies to overcome resistance from individuals who may feel threatened by the innovation

- Maintaining of momentum through the ups and downs that plague organizational life: personnel changes, expanding and shrinking budgets, and so forth

Early Tests of Business Potential

Stage Gates and Quick Kills

Key Topics Covered in This Chapter

- *The idea funnel*

- *Stage-gate systems—and a caution on using them*

- *Financial concept that innovators should understand*

- *Discovery-driven planning*

- *The R-W-W method for probing assumptions*

NOT EVERY IDEA whose commercial potential is recognized makes the challenging journey from concept to the marketplace. Even after passing the rough cut business evaluation described in chapter 3, subsequent development finds many—if not most—to be either technically infeasible, too costly to execute, or not acceptable to customers. By one estimate, only one in three thousand raw ideas will result in a commercial success.[1] The high idea mortality rate along the development path is a fact of life that innovative companies accept. They recognize the importance of culling weak and inappropriate ideas. They also recognize the need to have plenty of ideas in the pipeline if they want to maintain a modest degree of enterprise growth. Research on consumer goods companies, for example, has found that to achieve 3 percent annual growth, a $10 billion company must maintain a pipeline of innovation projects worth $5 billion.[2]

This chapter examines practices used by leading companies to determine which ideas they will kill and which they will place their bets on and support through development and commercialization.

The Idea Funnel

Innovative companies must eliminate unpromising ideas as quickly as possible, before they absorb significant resources. Even those that pass the opportunity recognition tests described in chapters 3 and 4 must be screened to identify the strongest and most promising. Learning more about an idea always involves costs—for staff people, for testing, for market research, and so forth. So the quicker they can kill off the ideas that won't make it to commercialization, the less their costs will be. Quick kills have the virtue of making more resources available for the handful of ideas that have real merit.

This notion of quickly killing off weak ideas, however, is easier said than done, and involves the risk of killing what might otherwise turn into gaming-changing products, services, or processes.

Product developers and academics have long used the *idea funnel* as a metaphor for the idea-filtering chore just described. The funnel shown in figure 5-1 has a wide mouth into which many undeveloped and roughly screened ideas are entered. The funnel narrows as the criteria for staying in the funnel become progressively more rigorous. Rigor takes the form of "tinkering," experimentation, market research, and prototyping. Some ideas survive this winnowing process longer than others. But only a few pass entirely through the tunnel toward commercialization.

FIGURE 5-1

The idea funnel

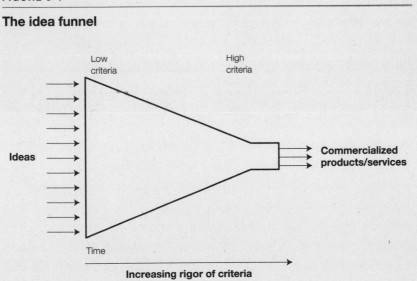

The funnel concept raises a number of important issues for innovators:

- What should be the criteria for staying in the funnel?

- How long will development and experimentation be allowed to progress before someone pushes the "kill" button?

- How should kill decisions be made?

There are no absolutely right or wrong answers to any of these questions. But different answers produce different consequences. For example, a company that allows ideas to remain in the funnel for a long time—that is, one that gives ideas every chance to prove themselves—is less likely to mistakenly kill a good idea. However, R&D costs will be higher than those tallied by a "quick kill" company. The slow-to-kill company will also take longer to get its winners out of the funnel and into commercialization, everything else being equal. This lengthens the entire product/service development process, which generally has negative consequences. Here's the reason: a company has a limited number of people available to evaluate and develop new ideas. The longer it takes these people to evaluate and dispose of an idea, the longer the remaining ideas will sit in the queue. That adds to total cycle time.[3]

On the other hand, allowing some ideas to remain in the funnel for a long time and supporting their gradual development with people-time and cash has been a winning strategy for some companies. The example of Corning, with its long period of experimentation with new concepts such as fiber optics and heat-resistant glass (Pyrex), has rewarded shareholders immensely over the decades.

The quick-kill company, in contrast, will reduce time and cost in its total development cycle. But its haste in disposing of many innovative ideas may result in accidentally killing a great idea that people simply do not understand. And the probability of making this mistake is greatest with the most innovative ideas, which require more effort to evaluate. A quick-kill approach may also alienate people the company depends on to feed the funnel with good ideas.

They may stop submitting new ideas if they see their ideas rejected "before their time." Quick kills may confirm the popular notion that the business people who control resources have a short-term view of innovation.

Thus, every company must keep one eye on its pool of good ideas and the other on its resources—funds, development personnel, market researchers, and so forth. And it must develop a workable balance in how it rejects some ideas and moves others forward. This balancing act is addressed in chapter 10.

Stage-Gates

The idea funnel is a useful way to conceptualize how a great number of innovative ideas are reduced to the handful with the greatest chance of commercial success. But which innovative ideas should remain in the funnel, and which should be allowed to proceed through it? Is there a practical method for deciding which ideas should be killed and which should move forward?

Every company must have a method for sorting good ideas from bad ones. For many companies that method is the stage-gate system. The *stage-gate system* was developed by Robert Cooper in the late 1980s.[4] It is an alternating series of development stages and assessment "gates" that aims for early elimination of weak ideas and faster time-to-market for potential winners. These stages and gates are generally organized around issues of feasibility, development, and launch. Figure 5-2 is a generic representation of that system. Here's how it works in practice:

- **Stage:** Stages are phases of the process during which development work is done. For example, a system would have stages for developing the raw idea, technical specifications, a prototype, and so forth. Commercialization is the final stage.

- **Gates:** Gates are checkpoints where people with decision-making authority determine if the project should be (1) killed,

FIGURE 5-2

A stage-gate system

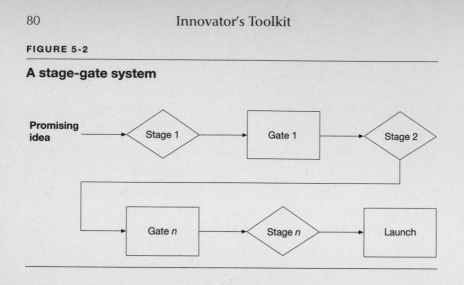

(2) sent back for more work, or (3) advanced to the next development stage. Gates may be used at various points to determine strategic fit, whether the project passes technical and financial hurdles, whether it's ready for prototyping, market testing or launch, and so forth.

A system like this is certainly an improvement over one that is either ad hoc or arbitrary. And for innovators it is certainly superior to a system in which they must curry favor with powerful executives to keep their projects alive and moving forward. It is also better for companies since, if managed properly, it prevents projects of dubious value from hanging on and soaking up scare resources that could be applied profitably elsewhere. Many companies have those types of projects. And they generally persist because there is no rational system for terminating them. This is where a stage-gate system can help.

The stage-gate system, however, is only as effective as the decision-making teams that control each gate. These teams should be composed of people who:

- Are experienced with innovation and product development

- Have expertise in the discipline required at their particular gate (e.g., marketing or financial analysis)

- Have the authority to extend or withdraw funding

- Are very clear about company strategy

- Understand the capacity of the company to connect certain types of products or services with customer markets

- Are objective and unencumbered by political pressure

- Are accountable for their decisions

You can probably imagine how the wrong people at various gates could undermine this system. The "wrong" people would be those who lack expertise or experience, are there to exert political pressure, or are out of touch with the market or company strategy. Top management should keep these people off their decision teams.

The first gate in any stage-gate system is the screening of what appear to be promising ideas. For the purposes of this book, screening is the most important gate since those that follow are clearly in the domain of new-product development, which is outside the scope of this discussion. There is no formula for idea screening, but an article by Robert Cooper suggests that screeners should do the following:

- **Seek a balance between errors of acceptance and rejection.** Don't be so conservative that only "sure things" are accepted, and don't be so lax that the company must spread its limited development funds too thinly over many projects. A proper balance must be employed.

- **Learn to live with ambiguity and uncertainty.** Reliable data and quantitative measures are almost never available at this early stage. Thus, gatekeepers who insist on cash flow projections and the revenue/expense minutia on which they are based should be patient.[5]

Add these steps to Cooper's suggested list:

- **Discuss the assumptions on which success will depend.** Those assumptions might include success in solving a technical problem, competitor passivity, and so forth.

- **Determine how the idea, if successful, would fit with the strategic goals of the company.** Innovation ideas must fit within the boundaries of a company's strategy to be successful.

A Caution on Funnels and Stage–Gates

Any process that helps a company sift through its innovative ideas and place its bets on the ones with the greatest potential must be used with extreme caution since it could, in the long run, put the company on the downward slope toward obsolescence. This caution is underscored by Clayton Christensen's warning that many high-performing companies have well-developed systems for killing ideas and products that their customers don't want. Funnels and stage gates are among them. "It's part of an entrenched philosophy that focuses resources on the most lucrative markets of the moment. As a result, these companies find it very difficult to invest in disruptive technologies—low margin opportunities that their customers don't want at that time—until their customers realize they want them. And by then it's too late."[6]

This is not to condemn funnels and stage-gate systems per se. These systems may be perfectly serviceable for both incremental innovations that serve existing markets and radical innovations that create new ones. The problem, some companies find, is with the screeners and the go/kill criteria they apply. If they kill every idea that cannot demonstrate value for existing customers or large existing markets (or that will disrupt their own profits; see "Cannibalization Issues"), then few radical ideas will survive. That will practically guarantee that the company will not be on the leading edge of the next wave of innovation that washes through its industry. Persistent killing of radical ideas will also signal to employees that the company is not interested in doing anything substantially different than what it has done in the past. They will tell themselves, "Wasting our time and resources on far-out ideas won't help our careers at this firm."

One antidote to this problem is to set up a parallel evaluation system to deal with innovations that fall outside the company's current

Cannibalization Issues

In many cases of innovation—both radical and incremental—development and commercialization of the idea will "cannibalize" some part of the company's existing business. For example, Toyota's hybrid power-source vehicle, the Prius, has attracted a number of buyers with strong interests in the environment and/or fuel economy. Based on positive auto reviews and praise from owners, sales of the Prius are likely to grow in the years ahead. We can assume that some number of these sales will be made to individuals who would have purchased existing Toyota models had the innovative hybrid car not been available. Thus a certain amount of cannibalization of existing sales will occur.

Innovators and managers must confront the cannibalization issue as they assess the value of their new technologies and products. In most cases they will conclude that the wisest course is to displace their own current products and services, otherwise competitors will step in to do the job.

markets and technologies. That system might have stage-gates, but its gatekeeping teams would be staffed by individuals with broader interests, long horizons, a solid sense of technological trends, successful track records as innovators or entrepreneurs, and status in the organization. These teams would be empowered to provide support to the best of these ideas. As we'll see in chapter 10, every company should have a portfolio that accommodates a reasonable number of long-shot but potentially game-changing ideas.

Financial Issues

Managers and innovators must eventually confront the financial issues bound up in new ideas. As stated earlier, measuring ideas with financial yardsticks in the earliest stage should be avoided. However, as those ideas move from one stage to another and progress closer and closer to commercialization, financial questions must be asked, including:

- How much will it cost to bring the idea to market?

- What price could the company reasonably ask for the innovative product or service?

- How many units could it expect to sell at that price?

- What costs of marketing, production, and service will be involved?

In its early stages, a radical idea is usually too raw and unformed to examine in terms of these questions. If the idea represents something truly new to the world, any answers would have to be based on sheer guesswork—hence, they would be useless.

The same cannot always be said of incremental innovations. By definition, an incremental innovation is simply a step or two removed from an existing product or service with a measurable market and pricing structure. Furthermore, the cost of developing the new idea, launching it, and filling orders can often be estimated from past experience with related products. Thus innovators and managers can often apply financial tools as they determine which ideas should move forward, be killed, or be sent back for additional development. Two of those tools are explained here: breakeven analysis and discounted cash flow analysis.

Breakeven Analysis

Breakeven analysis tells you how much (or how much more) you need to sell in order to pay for a fixed investment—in other words, at what point you will break even on the cash flow produced by a new product or service. With that information in hand, you can look at market demand and competitors' market shares to determine whether it's realistic to expect to sell that much. Breakeven analysis can also help you think through the impact of price changes and volume relationships.

More specifically, the breakeven calculation helps you determine the volume level at which the total after-tax contribution from a product or an investment covers its total fixed costs. But before you can perform the calculation, you need to understand the components that go into it:

- **Fixed costs:** These are costs that stay mostly the same, no matter how many units of a product or service are sold—costs such as insurance, management salaries, and rent or lease payments. For example, the rent on the production facility will be the same whether the company makes ten thousand or twenty thousand units, and so will the insurance.

- **Variable costs:** Variable costs are those that change with the number of units produced and sold; examples include utilities, labor, and the costs of raw materials. The more units you make, the more you consume these items.

- **Contribution margin:** This is the amount of money that every sold unit contributes to paying for fixed costs. It is defined as the net unit revenue minus variable (or direct) costs per unit.

With these concepts understood, we can make the calculation. We are looking for the solution to this straightforward equation:

Breakeven Volume = Fixed Costs/Unit Contribution Margin

And here's how you do it. First, find the unit contribution margin by subtracting the variable costs per unit from the net revenue per unit. Then divide total fixed costs, or the amount of the investment, by the unit contribution margin. The quotient is the breakeven volume, that is, the number of units that must be sold in order for all fixed costs to be covered.

To see breakeven analysis in practice, let's imagine that you have an idea for a new and improved version of your company's vegetable-processing machine. After some investigation, you estimate that the company will incur $500,000 in fixed costs in developing the tooling and production lines needed to manufacture this machine. That $500,000 cost will be the same whether the company produces one new and improved vegetable processor or one million. Meanwhile, the marketing people believe that each machine should sell for $75, and the manufacturing department estimates that the variable cost per unit will be $22. Then

$75 (price per unit) – $22 (variable cost per unit) =
$53 (unit contribution cargin)

therefore

$500,000 (total fixed cost)/$53 (unit contribution margin) =
9,434 units

The preceding calculations indicate that the company must sell 9,434 vegetable processors to recover its $500,000 investment. (But it's not always so simple; see "A Breakeven Complication.")

At this point, the company must decide whether the breakeven volume is achievable: is it realistic to expect to sell 9,434 veggie processors, and if so, how quickly?

Discounted Cash Flow

The second financial tool worth considering in this context is *discounted cash flow* (DCF) *analysis*. DCF is based on time-value-of-money concepts that recognize that a dollar received in the future is worth less than a dollar received today. For example, $1.03 received a year from today is worth only $1 if you received it today. Why? Because a dollar received today could be placed in a risk-free bank account paying 3 percent annual interest. In a year, you'd have $1.03. You understand compound interest; so think of DCF as reverse compounding. What does this have to do with innovation? A great deal. DCF analysis is a tool that CFOs, MBAs, and other people with business training use to evaluate the potential of ideas, projects, and investments. It's often the finger on the trigger that determines whether an innovative project is given the coup de grâce or allowed to live another day.

A Breakeven Complication

The veggie processor breakeven analysis represents a simple case. It assumes that costs are distinctly fixed or variable, that costs and unit contributions will not change as a function of volume (i.e., that the sale price of the item under consideration will not change at different levels of output). These assumptions may not hold in the real world. Rent, for example, may be fixed to a certain level of production, then increase by 30 percent as you rent a secondary facility to handle expanded output. Labor costs may in reality be a hybrid of fixed and variable costs. And as you push more and more of your product into the market, you may find it necessary to offer price discounts—which reduces contribution per unit. You will need to adjust the breakeven calculation to accommodate these untidy realities.

The above example of money received also introduced a number of important concepts used in DCF analysis that innovators and R&D people should understand. The $1 is a present value (PV)—that is, an amount received today. The $1.03 is a *future value* (FV)—the amount to which a present value, or series of payments, will increase over a specific period at a specific compounding rate. The number of periods (n) in this example is one year. And the rate (i)—sometimes called the *discount rate*—is 3 percent. When innovators understand these terms, they are on their way to speaking the same language that senior managers use when they decide to direct or withhold resources from innovative ideas. And with a little help from a financial calculator or a preprogrammed electronic spreadsheet, it's possible to calculate present values and future values with ease.

(*Note:* If these concepts are new to you, and if you'd like to learn more, see *Harvard Business Essential: Finance for Managers.* It explains time value concepts, how to calculate them, and provides several examples. You'll find similar material in any finance textbook.)

DCF has many applications in business decision making. Let's consider one that involves a project based on incremental innovation:

"The 'IdiotFones' Case"

Rhoda and her team submitted a proposal to Acme Communications' innovation assessment committee to develop a new line of cell phones with built-in global positioning satellite (GPS) capabilities. "Thanks to this new product," said the proposal, "people who talk incessantly on their cell phones while driving will no longer need to keep track of where they are going—a serious problem for 83 percent of people who use cell phones in their vehicles, according to our research. By simply pushing the GPS button on their new 'IdiotFones,' these confused individuals will be able to determine their exact locations at any time of the day or night. Another phone button will automatically dial 911 for emergency service when and if they strike pedestrians while taking those all-important calls."

Acme's senior managers were impressed. But they wondered if the IdiotFone was a good financial bet. Rhoda's team addressed their concern with DCF analysis based on estimates of fixed development costs, manufacturing costs, marketing and selling costs, and anticipated revenues. That analysis, shown in table 5-1, involved a multiyear series of cash flows discounted to their present values using Acme's *cost of capital* (10 percent) as the discount rate. When discounted to the present and summed, the positive cash flows produced over the first five years exceeded the up-front investment even as it earned its cost of capital, making the IdiotFone proposal something worthy of management attention.

(*Note:* To find the present value of a particular future cash flow, you need to know the *amount* of the cash flow, the number of *years* you must wait to receive it, and the *discount rate*. Once you have these, any financial calculator or computer spreadsheet will calculate it for you. Or simply go online to a site such as

TABLE 5-1

Net present value of IdiotFone cash flow*

Year	0	1	2	3	4	5
Cash flows	-400	+50	+70	+100	+150	+200
PV	-400	+45.45	+57.85	+75.13	+102.45	+124.18
NPV (sum of PVs 0 through 5)					+5.067 or	$5,067

* In thousands; discount rate = 10 percent

http://www.moneychimp.com/calculator/present_value_calculator.htm, input the numbers and let it do the work for you. Or calculate it directly using the formula PV = cash flow/ $(1 - \text{discount rate})^n$, where n is the number of years between the present and the year in which the cash flow is received.)

This simplified example foresees a negative cash flow of $400,000 in year zero—Acme's upfront investment in IdiotFone development and tooling. This is the cash outflow required to get the project off the ground. The company then experiences a positive cash flow of $50,000 *at the end* of the first year, as revenues from phone sales kick in. Larger cash flows follow as IdiotFones become more popular.

To find the *net present value* of Acme's stream of cash flows, one must find the present value of each of the positive cash flows, discounted at 10 percent for the appropriate number of years. Adding together those present values and then subtracting the $400,000 initially invested yields the net present value of the investment. As long as that net value is positive, the project earns its cost of capital and more.

USE DFC WITH CARE. Discounted cash flow is a powerful analytical tool. But it must be used with care. The final calculation is only as good as the numbers that go into it. In the IdiotFone example, one would ask:

- Where did the $400,000 investment cost come from? How accurate is it? Won't ongoing investment be required to keep the new product line going?

- How accurate are the cash flow estimates for years 1 through 5? Did the project team consult with experienced marketing and manufacturing personnel in developing these numbers?

- What is the level of uncertainty associated with each cash flow estimate? If the estimates are the median value in a range of possible estimates, what are the high and low estimates for each range?

Decision makers would also want to know their alternatives to this investment. Even if they accepted the proposal and its DCF analysis at face value, prudence would dictate that it be considered in the context of competing projects.

Clayton Christensen and two colleagues cautioned managers of the potential dangers of DCF and other methods of financial analysis in a 2008 article aptly titled, "Innovation Killers: How Financial Tools Destroy Your Capacity to Do New Things."[7] In their view, the use of discounted cash flow and net present value causes decision makers to underestimate the real returns and benefits of radical (or disruptive) innovation. Among the problems they cite is the difficulty of estimating future cash flows from truly innovative projects. "Numbers for the 'out years,'" they write, "can be a complete shot in the dark." Cash flow projections for incremental projects, in comparison, are bound to be more reliable and, thus, more comforting and acceptable to management. The result is that incremental projects get a green light while truly innovative projects are more likely to get the axe. Being smart people, engineers and product developers quickly learn that project champions who tout the grandest cash flow forecasts usually win this game, and adjust their forecasts upward.

Christensen and his coauthors also make the point that decision makers too often assume that the enterprise's overall revenues will

FIGURE 5-3

The DCF trap

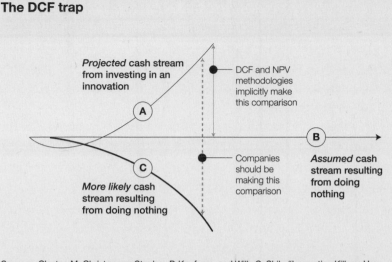

Projected cash stream from investing in an innovation

A

DCF and NPV methodologies implicitly make this comparison

B

C

Companies should be making this comparison

Assumed cash stream resulting from doing nothing

More likely cash stream resulting from doing nothing

Source: Clayton M. Christensen, Stephen P. Kaufamn, and Willy C. Shih, "Innovation Killers: How Financial Tools Destroy Your Capacity to Do New Things," *Harvard Business Review*, January 2008. With permission.

continue on a steady trajectory if they do not invest in innovative projects. In this line of thinking, which they call "the DCF Trap," a successful project will add to overall revenues; doing nothing will leave revenues unchanged. The more likely scenario, in their view, is a decline in enterprise revenues if innovation investments are not made (figure 5-3).

Discovery-Driven Planning

Another approach to making decisions on project investments is *discovery-driven planning*, the brainchild of Rita Gunther McGrath and Ian MacMillian. In their approach, decision makers and project teams focus their attention on the assumptions that must prove true if the venture or innovation is to reach a level of profitability acceptable to management. These assumptions are more critical than estimated cash flow numbers, the centerpiece of the DCF approach. Their system operates with the view that "little is known and that much is assumed."[8] In this sense, the traditional DCF approach may be most applicable to products and services that people already understand and have experience with, whereas the discovery-driven planning approach may be more effective in dealing with ventures for which there are no handy models.

McGrath and MacMillan advocate a method that begins "at the end," with the minimally acceptable net profits needed to make the venture worthwhile—say €1 million in net profits. Using profits as the starting point, decision makers then work backward to determine the revenues required to make that profit possible. In reaching this figure, they must consider all the activities required to produce, sell, service, and deliver the new product or service to customers.

The focus then shifts to all the assumptions behind profits, revenue, and allowable costs. "Can we assume that people will pay €50 retail for the item?" "Is it reasonable to think that unit manufacturing cost will come in under €12?"

The R–W–W Method

An alternative approach to probing the underlying assumptions of an innovative idea is the R–W–W method: Is it *R*eal? Can we *W*in? Is it *W*orth doing? This practical approach was described by Wharton professor George Day in a 2007 article.[9]

The method requires people to investigate three lines of inquiry:

1. **Is it real?** In answering this question, managers and idea champions must determine if a market for the innovative idea exists. It exists only if:

   • Target customers have a need or desire for the product or service

   • They have the financial capacity to purchase the ultimate product or service

- There are enough potential buyers
- Consumers will buy (for instance, they are willing to switch from an existing competitor)

2. **Can we win?** This question must be answered both in terms of the product or service and in terms of the company itself. The *product/service* will be competitive if:

- It offers clear advantages over alternatives
- Its advantages are sustainable (as through patents, etc.)
- It can survive responses by competitors (such as competitor price cutting)

The *company* will be competitive if:

- It has superior resources (e.g., lower-cost manufacturing, engineering, etc.)
- The company and its people have experience in the market and skills appropriate for the project's scale and complexity
- The innovative idea's champion and sponsors can energize people and senior management around the project and its successful execution
- Insights gained from customers by market researchers and other customer contacts are shared freely with development team members.

3. **Is it worth it?** This is another two-part question. The first part concerns strategic fit, the second is financial. For truly radical innovation, the financial question may be the most difficult to answer, since the horizons for these innovations are the most clouded. Nevertheless, the ultimate product or service will be worth doing—that is, will be profitable at an acceptable level of risk—if forecasted returns are greater than forecasted cost, considering the timing and amounts of capital outlays, marketing expenses, delivery costs, and so forth.

Answers to R–W–W questions will most likely fall on a continuum from a clear yes to a clear no. Author–scholar Day suggests that development teams work together to reach consensus on them. Figure 5-4, from his article, summarizes a complete set of R–W–W questions.

FIGURE 5-4

R-W-W screening questions

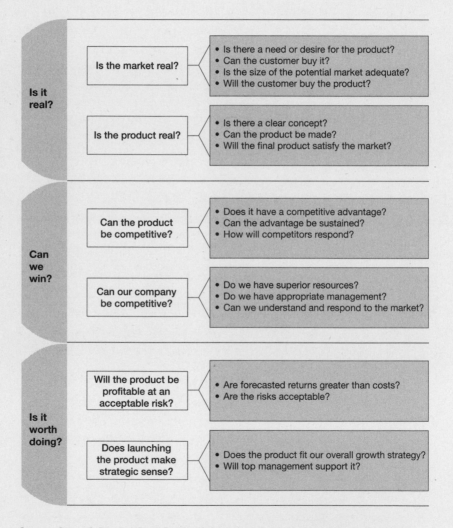

Is it real?	Is the market real?	• Is there a need or desire for the product? • Can the customer buy it? • Is the size of the potential market adequate? • Will the customer buy the product?
	Is the product real?	• Is there a clear concept? • Can the product be made? • Will the final product satisfy the market?
Can we win?	Can the product be competitive?	• Does it have a competitive advantage? • Can the advantage be sustained? • How will competitors respond?
	Can our company be competitive?	• Do we have superior resources? • Do we have appropriate management? • Can we understand and respond to the market?
Is it worth doing?	Will the product be profitable at an acceptable risk?	• Are forecasted returns greater than costs? • Are the risks acceptable?
	Does launching the product make strategic sense?	• Does the product fit our overall growth strategy? • Will top management support it?

Source: George S. Day, "Is It Real? Can We Win? Is It Worth Doing: Managing Risk and Reward in an Innovation Portfolio," *Harvard Business Review*, December 2007.

Summing Up

This chapter examined the final phase of the innovation process: moving ideas to the market. In this phase companies must develop a rational approach to rejecting some of the ideas developed earlier and moving others forward—toward eventual commercialization. The idea funnel and stage-gate systems were put forth:

- The funnel is not a method but a conceptual framework that describes what must go on as innovative ideas are moved toward commercialization. By degrees and through rational processes, many ideas are reduced to the most commercially promising few.

- The stage-gate system, an alternating series of development stages and assessment "gates," aims for early elimination of weak ideas and faster time-to-market for potential winners. These stages and gates control events from the initial idea all the way to commercialization.

The chapter also discussed the financial tolls that become important as an innovative idea moves closer to commercialization. Two assessment methods were described:

- **Breakeven analysis:** This is a quantitative measure of how many units will have to be sold at a given net price and assuming fixed and variable costs for the organization to break even.

- **Discounted cash flow (DCF) analysis:** This is a method for determining the monetary value of a commercialized idea over a particular span of time based on time-value-of-money concepts. The effectiveness of this methodology will be only as good as the assumptions used.

Finally, the chapter introduced two methods for evaluating innovative projects: discovery-driven planning and R-W-W. The first is an alternative to traditional stage-gate and DCF analyses; it focuses the attention of decision makers on the assumptions—and not the cash flow projections—that would have to be correct in order for a venture or innovation to be financially acceptable. This approach is likely to be more useful in situations that have no immediate comparables, such as a new-to-the-world innovation, business model, or business. The second method, R–W–W, can be used with the stage-gate method.

6

Types of Strategy

Which Fits Your Business?

Key Topics Covered in This Chapter

- *Low-cost leadership strategy, and how to make it work*

- *Differentiating a product or service—even a commodity—in ways that create real value for customers*

- *Customer relationship strategy, and six approaches for making it valuable for customers*

- *The network effect strategy: winner-take-all*

- *Determining which strategic approach is right for you*

NOW THAT WE'VE considered the issues surrounding types of innovations and sources of innovative ideas, how you can recognize and gain support for them, and what management can do to separate good ideas from bad, it's time to consider their strategic implications.

Look at the many textbooks on business strategy and you'll find a cornucopia of strategy frameworks: low-cost leadership, diversification, merger-acquisition, global, customer focus, product leadership, vertical integration, flexibility, product/service differentiation, and so forth. What are these strategies? And now that you understand the external environment and your internal strengths and weaknesses, how can you determine which is best and most appropriate for your company?

At bottom, every for-profit entity aims for the same goal: to identify and pursue a strategy that will give it a defensible and profitable hold on some segment of the marketplace. That segment, by choice, may be large or small. It may produce, by choice, high profits on a small number of transactions, or low profits on every one of millions of sales. It may involve superficial relationships with many customers or long-term and deep relationships with just a few. No matter which strategies they follow, these companies will also try to increase the range of profitability—that is, the difference between what customers are willing to pay and the company's cost of providing its goods or services.

This chapter describes four basic strategies: low-cost leadership; product/service differentiation, customer relationship, and the network effect. It is difficult to find a business strategy that is not one of these or some variation. Chances are that your innovative idea will fit into one of them.

Low-Cost Leadership

Low-cost leadership has paved the road to success for many companies. Discount retailers in the United States such as E.J. Korvette and later Kmart grabbed significant chunks of the retail market away from traditional department stores and specialty stores when they first appeared in the 1950s and 1960s. Their success was a function of their ability to deliver goods at lower prices; and they developed that ability by keeping their cost structures much lower than those of traditional competitors. These early discounters were displaced, in turn, by Wal-Mart and Target, which were even more effective in operating a low-cost strategy. Wal-Mart's success, in part, stems from its innovations in supply chain management.

In this strategy, the product or service is usually the same as the product or service offered by rivals. It may be a commodity, such as rolled steel or electrical wire, or it may be something readily available through other vendors. Items sold by Wal-Mart, for example, can be obtained at many other locations, some just down the street—Duracell batteries, Minolta binoculars, Canon cameras, Kodak photographic film, Wrangler jeans, Hanes underwear, Gillette razor blades, Bic pens. So why do so many people in North America head to Wal-Mart to buy these items, often driving past rival vendor locations? Because they believe they will get the same items for less money. And they usually do.

The key to success using the low-cost strategy is to deliver the customer's expected level of value at a cost that assures an adequate level of profitability. Consider figure 6-1, which is adapted from a model first advanced by Adam Brandenburger and Harborne Stuart.[1] The vertical distance between the willingness of customers to pay (top line) and the cost of providing the product itself (bottom line) represents the range of pricing within which every company

FIGURE 6-1

Expected value

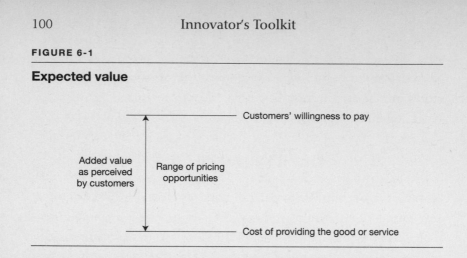

must operate. It also represents the value added by the company, as perceived by customers. For commoditylike or undifferentiated products, the spread between these lines is narrow. And the top line—what customers are willing to pay—is generally fixed, particularly when competition is strong. So, to establish greater profitability, the vendor must push the cost-of-providing line lower. It will generally attempt to do this through operational efficiency, pressuring suppliers for low prices, and other means. This is the game that Wal-Mart has been playing and winning for many years. It has squeezed more costs out of its supply chain than any other major retailer.

Using process innovation that automates data from the checkout register back to product suppliers—to the suppliers' suppliers—Wal-Mart's supply chain technology managed to break the "three-day barrier," a feat that many in the retail trade had thought impossible. Using information technology, Wal-Mart is often able to move replenishment items from suppliers to its shore shelves (not to its own warehouses) in less than three days. Thus, when a customer buys a toaster oven at the Wal-Mart store in Lynn, Massachusetts, the purchase triggers a signal that "pulls" a replacement item to that store's shelf. Rapid turnaround makes it possible for the company to maintain lower levels of inventory than competitors while meeting customer demand—and saving millions in working capital. Lower store inventories also make it possible to offer greater product diversity in the same floor space. Rapid supplier response also puts Wal-Mart stores in a better position to respond to unanticipated demand and changing customer requirements. The fact that the entire system is automated reduces the labor costs that burden so many retailers.

It's easy to assume that the low-cost leadership strategy applies solely to physical products: jeans, paint, tons of steel, and so forth. There are, however, many examples of low-cost strategy in the service sector. Consider The Vanguard Group, a leading investment management company. Started in 1974 by John Bogle, the company provides a broad array of mutual funds and a very high level of client service. There is nothing particularly fancy about Vanguard or its funds. While some of its actively managed funds have been top performers over the long term, many are index funds that purposely aim to replicate the return of the market, not "beat" it. In most years, these passive index funds actually outperform the average managed funds in the same category. Index funds require very little human tending and operate without benefit of highly paid securities analysts and portfolio managers. The index fund is an innovation whose roots are found in financial academic research and its practical application by pioneering portfolio managers such as Charles Ellis in the 1970s. Bogle recognized the value of index funds and successfully popularized it among individual investors.

What also sets Vanguard apart from other fund families is its no-commission policy and the fact that it has the lowest average expense ratio among fund families. In 2003, for example, Vanguard's average expense ratio was a tiny 0.25 percent of assets—less than one-fifth of the mutual fund industry's average expense ratio of 1.38 percent. That has the effect of giving Vanguard clients a 1.13 percent greater annual return on their money (all else being equal). By keeping management and transaction costs low, Vanguard actually invests and reinvests more of a client's money. And that produces better returns over time, all other factors being equal. Vanguard's success with this strategy has earned it accolades among individual investors and made it one of the largest fund families in the United States.

Making the Low-Cost Strategy Work

As mentioned above, the key to retaining low-cost leadership is keeping the costs of providing goods or services lower than those of competitors. This is a constant challenge, since rivals will be working hard to drive their costs lower than yours. But it can be achieved through several means, and innovation—bother process and product (or service) innovation—can play a role in several. Consider these four:

CONTINUOUS IMPROVEMENT IN OPERATING EFFICIENCY. The Japanese developed the philosophy of *kaizen*, or continuous process improvement, to gain their well-known lead in manufacturing. *Kaizen* encourages all members of the organization, from the executive suite to the loading dock, to seek out ways to incrementally improve what they are doing. It has a lot in common with incremental innovation, as described in chapter 1. A 1 percent improvement here and a 2 percent improvement there quickly add up over time, giving the firm a notable cost advantage. The concept of *process reengineering* aims for a similar result, but *kaizen* aims for incremental improvements to the existing work, whereas process engineering aims for breakthrough change—either through wholesale restructuring or the total elimination of existing activities. Process reengineering is a form of reinvention. Both *kaizen* and process engineering have had profound impacts of operating efficiency in both manufacturing and services.

EXPLOITATION OF THE EXPERIENCE CURVE. Production managers know that people learn to do the same job more quickly and with fewer errors the more frequently they do the job. Thus, a heart operation that once took eight hours can be completed successfully in four hours as a surgical team gains more and more experience with the procedure. And before long, the procedure may take the team only two or three hours. The same pattern is observed in manufacturing settings in which managers and employees focus on learning.

The *experience curve* concept holds that the cost of doing a repetitive task decreases by some percentage each time the cumulative volume of production doubles. Thus, a company that gets onto the experience curve sooner than an imitator can theoretically maintain a cost advantage. Consider the two cost curves in figure 6-2. Both companies A and B begin at the same cost level and learn at the same rate. They compete primarily on price. But A got into the business first and, consequently, is further down the cost curve than rival B, maintaining its cost advantage at every point in time. At time T, for instance, that advantage is C. Company B must either learn at a much faster rate, accept a permanent cost disadvantage (and smaller profit margin), or exit the market.

AN UNBEATABLE SUPPLY CHAIN. Wal-Mart is not the only master player of the supply chain strategy. Everyone is familiar with the Dell business model. It sells its PCs directly to consumers, skipping the middleman. It also builds those PCs to order, thus eliminating the costly finished goods inventory problem that plagues rivals that operate with traditional business models. It has no finished products sitting on the shelf and becoming technologically obsolete with each passing day.

FIGURE 6-2

The experience curve

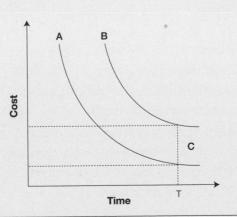

What people often overlook about Dell is the innovativeness of its efficient and effective supply chain. That chain includes component suppliers, assemblers, and the logistical services of UPS. All are digitally linked so that order information can be immediately translated into production and delivery schedules. The ability of this supply chain to deliver a customized PC to a customer's doorstep in a week or so makes it possible to eliminate middlemen and inventory costs, giving the company cost leadership in its field.

PRODUCT INNOVATION. Huge cost reductions are often achieved through product innovation. For example, back in the 1970s, Black & Decker, a manufacturer of consumer power tools, found itself going head-to-head with low-cost Asian competitors. It had a serious cost disadvantage that could not be cured simply by being more thrifty and efficient. Something more dramatic was required. B&D responded with product innovation—it redesigned its entire family of consumer power tools *and* the process for making them. At the heart of this product line makeover was a new electric motor that could be inexpensively altered to provide power for any number of different hand tools. That eliminated dozens of different motor types as well as the need to make and store hundreds of different components. The core product platform's simplicity and "manufacturability" made it possible to produce the new family of tools with 85 percent lower labor costs. Inventory and other related costs tumbled by similar percentages. The Société Micromécanique et Horlogère (SMH) accomplished similar results with its development of Swatch watch, which was based on the company's development of a reliable, plastic, quartz timekeeper that could be mass-produced for a tiny fraction of the cost of traditional watch works. This design breakthrough made it possible for the Swiss company to compete and prosper in a market dominated by low-cost Asian competitors.

In these and other cases, product innovation or redesign proved to be an effective tool for achieving cost leadership.

Is a low-cost strategy feasible for your company? If it is, what would have to happen to make it work?

Differentiation

Every successful strategy is about *differentiation*, even the low-cost leadership strategy. "We can fly you to Barcelona for less than our competitors." "At Auto City Sales, we will not be undersold." But for most companies, differentiation is expressed in some qualitative way that customers value. For example, when Thomas Edison first began to market his system of electric incandescent lighting, his principal rivals were local gas companies. Both methods of illumination were effective, but Edison's approach had clear differences that most customers favored. Unlike gas lamps, Edison's innovative electric lighting didn't noticeably heat up people's living rooms on hot summer nights. It was more convenient, requiring just a flick of the switch to turn it on and off. And it eliminated a serious fire hazard in many applications, such as in small, closed spaces. Edison played on these qualitative differences as he attacked and eliminated the gas companies' dominance of urban lighting in the late 1800s and early 1900s.

Companies today likewise adopt differentiation strategies. Consider the auto industry. Volvo touts the crashworthiness of its vehicles to set itself apart. Toyota plays on its reputation for quality and high resale value; more recently it has differentiated its Prius model with high-mileage hybrid engine technology. The MINI Cooper practically screams "I'm fun to drive" to potential buyers. Porsche has also differentiated itself by concentrating on the development of high-performance sports cars—while GM may offer a vehicle for every household budget, and Toyota may claim a high level of quality and reliability, neither have much appeal for the small number of drivers who look for speed, agility, and a sense that they could handle the raceway circuit at LeMans. That is what Porsche aims to deliver through its strategy of differentiation.

Differentiating a Commodity Product

Even among commodity products, business strategists have found and exploited opportunities to differentiate themselves. Although price and product features may be identical, it is still possible to differentiate on the basis of service. The cement business provides an example. Cement is cement, right? That's the fact that Mexico-based CEMEX, the world's third-largest provider of cement, is faced with. Cement is a commodity product. Nevertheless, CEMEX has developed a strategy of fast and reliable delivery that qualitatively differentiates the company from its many rivals. As described by David Bovet and Joseph Martha in their book on supply chain excellence, CEMEX has become a major industry power in many markets because it adopted a production and high-tech logistics strategy that achieves on-time delivery 98 percent of the time, versus the 34 percent record of most competitors. For construction companies operating on tight schedules, that reliability is highly valued, especially when a late delivery means that dozens of highly paid crew members will be standing around doing nothing. "This super reliability" write Bovet and Martha, "allows [CEMEX] to charge a premium in most markets."[2] In this case, super reliability has effectively differentiated a commodity product. Something similar may be achieved by offering superior customer support.

Effective Differentiation

Is your company following a strategy of differentiation? If it is, what sets it apart from the products and services of rivals? Whatever the answer, remember that differentiation only matters to the extent that *customers value the difference*. Maybe not all customers, but the ones you have targeted. If these customers truly value that which sets your product or service apart, they will either (1) select your offering over those of others, (2) be willing to pay a premium for what you offer, or (3) act on some combination of 1 and 2. Experience and market research are the best ways to determine if your difference will be valued by customers.

Some companies have been more successful than others in using innovation to make their products stand out from the crowd in appealing ways. MP3 players and digital recording devices had been around for a while before Apple launched its initial iPod models. Thanks to an innovative user interface and the availability of music, podcasts, and movies through the iTunes Store, iPod stood out and became the market leader. The company struck again in late 2007, launching its innovative iPhone into a market crowded with other cell-phone vendors.

How could innovation successfully differentiate your product or service?

Customer Relationship

Everyone knows that you can buy a camera or wide-angle lens for less at Wal-Mart, Best Buy, or one of the other discount stores. But many people still patronize small, independently owned photography shops when they purchase cameras, accessories, and film. Likewise, Fantastic Sams, a national franchise, provides great hairstyling services at low prices, yet many—if not most—women will pay more to go to the stylist who has been handling their hair for the past many years. Many women, in fact, can claim a longer-term relationship with their male hairstylists than with their husbands! In the words of one, "A husband is replaceable—a good hairdresser isn't."

What's going on here? Why do so many customers pay more to patronize local camera shops, hairdressers, corner bookstores, neighborhood meat markets and bakeries, and many other vendors of goods and services when they could get a cheaper deal elsewhere? The reason is that they *value* the personal relationship experienced in doing business with these shops, their owners, and their employees. The relationship itself can take many forms: doing business with a familiar face; the fact that the vendor knows the customers and their needs; or the vendor's willingness to explain the product, how to use it, and the pros and cons of different purchase choices. It's difficult to find these qualities online, in a direct-mail catalog, or at most big-box stores. Those vendors provide a transaction, but not a relationship.

Relationship Strategy at Work: USAA

While big companies are at a disadvantage in building and executing a customer relationship strategy, it is not impossible, and innovation can often make the difference. Consider the case of USAA. Not many readers will have ever heard of this *Fortune* 500 financial services company, even though it has more than $75 billion under management. That's because it caters exclusively to a very small slice of the total U.S. population: active-duty and retired National Guard, and Army Reserve enlisted personnel; officers and officer candidates; and their dependents.

The people in USAA's target market, however, know the company very well, and a large percentage of them are customers of its banking, insurance, and credit card services. Among active-duty officers, participation is 90 to 95 percent. And because it is a mutual company, customers are also part owners.

After decades of serving this population, USAA understands its unique banking, insurance, and retirement needs. And it knows how to deal with the fact that military personnel are transferred from post to post and around the world with great frequency. Its understanding of customers is expressed in many ways that people appreciate. For example, when customers are deployed overseas or to a war zone, their cars are usually put in storage for one or more years; in these cases USAA urges them to request elimination of the costly liability component of their auto insurance policies. No other auto insurer would think to do that. And unlike other life insurers, its policies have no war clause provision. USAA customers know that full policy death benefits will be paid if they die for *any* reason, including wartime service.

USAA's close relationship with its military clientele and its understanding of their unique lifestyle can be traced back to its founding in 1922 by twenty-five army officers who found it difficult—owing to their profession and mobility—to obtain auto insurance. Even today, a substantial number of USAA executives and employees are former military people, and customer-serving employees are given extensive training on the unique financial needs of military personnel.[3] Personal service is their highest priority.

USAA focuses on a much narrower market segment than just about any other *Fortune* 500 company, but that focus and attention to customer relationships has paid off in terms of revenue growth, profitability, and customer satisfaction. In 2004, a poll of affluent investors put USAA at the top of financial services companies, with a satisfaction score 8 percent higher than TIAA-CREF, which also serves a highly focused market group, and 73 percent higher than Fidelity, which serves the general public. In 2007, a survey conducted by Forrester Research put the company at the top among financial services companies for customer advocacy, defined by that study as customers' perception that a company is doing what's best for them and not just for the company's profitability. Eighty-eight percent of the USAA customers surveyed said "My financial provider does what's best for me, not just its own bottom line." The next-highest vendor scored only 78 percent.[4]

Making the Customer Relationship Strategy Work

For a small company that deals face-to-face with its clientele, innovation may play no role in a customer relationship strategy. Those relationships are organic to the business. For a large corporation that has many thousands of employees scattered across the nation or around the globe, however, the quality of customer relationship must be baked into the entity's design, its customer interfaces, and the processes through which customers are served. In every case, one must find ways to create relationships that represents value to customers. That value can take many forms:

- **Simplifying customers' lives or work:** A USAA auto insurance holder does not have to obtain a new insurance policy every time he or she is transferred to another state—a common experience for military personnel.

- **Ongoing benefits:** Microsoft gains relationship points through its practice of notifying software users of critical updates, which can be downloaded without charge.

- **Personalized service:** Many top-tier hotels have developed personalized approaches to handling repeat visitors by storing check-in information and customer preferences in their companywide data bases. This enables express check-in, gives customers the service they want, and adds a personal touch: "Welcome back to XYZ Hotels, Mr. Jones. We have a nonsmoking room for you. Do you still prefer having the *Wall Street Journal* delivered with your continental breakfast?"

- **Customized solutions:** Rather than continue to sell one-size-fits-all products and service, innovative companies find ways to economically customize their offerings to the unique requirements of individual customers, building stronger personal connections to them.

- **Personal contact:** Instead of channeling incoming customer calls to whichever service rep is available, many companies now give every established customer an account representative; this puts a personal voice on what would otherwise be an impersonal transaction.

- **Continuous learning.** Many companies have adopted CRM (customer relationship management) techniques to better understand and serve their most loyal and profitable customers. CRM identifies contact points between customer and company, and views each as an opportunity to learn more about customer needs.

The Network Effect

When the first telephones were sold in the late nineteenth century, they weren't particularly useful. A person could only call one of the few other owners of the new gadget. But the telephone's utility grew as more and more homes, stores, and offices joined the telephone network. This is called the *network effect*—a phenomenon in which the value of a product increases as more products are sold and the network of users increases.

As a deliberate strategy, the network effect is fairly new. Perhaps its most obvious practitioner and beneficiary is eBay, the online auction company. eBay began as a hobby business of its founder, Pierre Omidyar, who developed software and an online system that allowed individuals to list new and used items of all types for auction. His wasn't the first online auction site, but it was the first to become widely popular, and that popularity sent the network effect into high gear. Buyers flocked to eBay over other sites because it had the most sellers, and sellers listed their items on eBay because it attracted the most buyers. This virtuous circle quickly established Omidyar's site as the dominant online auction site, and it continues to support eBay's remarkable growth.

There is no evidence that Omidyar and his colleagues set out with an implicit network effect strategy. It simply happened. However, early success encouraged them to use their rising tide of revenue to keep the ball rolling, which they did through heavy investments in site development, customer service, brand recognition, and a number of strategic acquisitions.

Success with a network strategy depends heavily on a company's ability to get out in front and become the dominant provider. Doing so leaves very little space available for challengers, which is why some call this a winner-take-all strategy. eBay quickly dominated its industry. Microsoft did the same with its Windows operating system, though most experienced computer users agree that the user-friendly Macintosh operating system developed by Apple is superior to Windows. But Apple kept its operating system proprietary, while Microsoft allowed its operating system to be installed on all PC manufacturers' machines. Thus, since most PCs operated with Windows, most new software was developed for Windows machines. And because most software was Windows-based, more people bought PCs equipped with the Windows operating system. To date, this virtuous circle appears to be unbroken.

. . .

This chapter has presented four general strategies. Each has been a winning ticket for any number of companies. Chances are that one or another—or some variation—would be appropriate for your company. But which one? Look for the answer in your company's mission, its goals, and what you have managed to learn through external and internal analysis, as shown in figure 6-3. Think of the mission as setting the boundaries within which you may seek a new strategy. Your goals set the bar of achievement that the strategy must be capable of attaining.

You should understand, however, that any strategic choice involves trade-offs. If you choose to focus on a narrow set of customers, as in the USAA example, you'll have to give up the idea of serving the broad general market. As Michael Porter has warned, "Companies that try to be all things to all customers . . . risk confusion in the trenches as employees attempt to make day-to-day operating decisions without a clear framework."[5] Thus, if you want to be the low-cost retailer in your field, don't try to set up a special boutique chain of stores to cater to high-end customers. You'll confuse the market and yourself.

FIGURE 6-3

Which strategy is best?

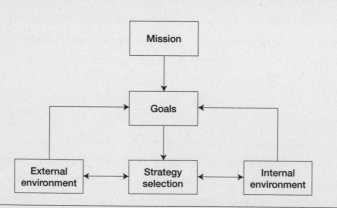

Above all, make sure that your choice of strategy is aligned with the primary customer market you plan to address. This may be the most critical factor in strategy creation. Keep your chosen customer market in your sights at all times, and make sure that your colleagues do the same. Alignment between strategy and customers is absolutely essential. And innovation in product, service, process, or customer delivery can help you win the game.

Summing Up

- As a strategy, low-cost leadership is most appropriate in industries in which competitors essentially offer a commoditylike product or service.

- Continuous improvement in operating efficiency, process reengineering, exploitation of the experience curve, supply chain power, and product innovation are among the methods used to achieve low-cost leadership.

- A differentiation strategy sets the product or service apart from those of rivals in a qualitative way.

- Commodity products—those with standard features, quality, and price—can be differentiated from those of rivals by means of faster, more reliable delivery and/or superior customer support.

- Strong customer relationships can be used to retain customers who would otherwise gravitate toward lower-cost providers.

- To be effective, a customer relationship strategy must provide something that customers value—for example, something that simplifies their lives or work, ongoing benefits, personalized service, or customized solutions.

- The network effect is a phenomenon in which the value of a product increases as more products are sold. Companies that pursue this strategy (or benefit from it) succeed to the extent

that they can get out in front and become the dominant
provider of some enabling product or service, such as eBay's
online auction site or Microsoft's Windows operating system.

• Whichever strategy type you consider, always look for alignment between the strategy and your target customer market.

Strategic Moves

Mechanisms for Market Entry and Dominance

Key Topics Covered in This Chapter

- *Gaining a beachhead in occupied terrain*

- *Using innovation to overcome barriers to entry*

- *Gaining market entry through product differentiation*

- *Creating and then dominating a new market*

- *Enlisting the power of product/service platform*

CHAPTER 6 IDENTIFIED the most common strategy types: low-cost leadership, product/service differentiation, customer relationship, and the network effect. It also pointed out instances in which innovation has helped companies apply them successfully.

There's much more to strategy than deciding which version or variant of these strategies is best for your company. This chapter continues the discussion, indicating how strategy can be used to enter and build defensible positions in the marketplace. It explores a number of potential strategic moves. The discussion here is selective owing to the "essentials" nature of this book. But they should get you thinking about what your company might accomplish.

Gaining a Market Beachhead

In his classic book on military strategy, *On War*, Carl von Clausewitz told his readers that "Where absolute superiority is not attainable, you must produce a relative one at the decisive point by making skillful use of what you have."[1] Von Clausewitz's advice reminds us that the strategist must reckon with the realities of the market and the existence of competing firms, some of which will have greater market power and financial resources. This means that one must strike in an area of competitor weakness, where the competitor is unlikely to fight back, or where it will fail to fight back effectively. The strategy chosen, then, must be made in view of this situation.

Consider the case of the U.S. auto industry during the 1960s and 1970s. None of the domestic automakers of the time were skilled at producing small, fuel-efficient vehicles. This was not the result of engineering ineptitude; there simply wasn't strong demand for small cars in the United States. Fuel prices relative to incomes were very low, and most consumers liked roomier vehicles. Also, profits on the few small cars made or sold in America—both in terms of margin and absolute dollars—were far lower than those obtained from larger vehicles. Detroit automakers said "Why bother?" to small cars. Lacking products from domestic producers, customers who wanted small cars gravitated toward small foreign manufacturers. The Volkswagen Beetle had already become something of a statement among students, the thrifty, and antiestablishment types. Before long, Datsun, Fiat, and Renault brought their small, economical vehicles to the low end of the huge U.S. market where they had, in Clausewitzian terms, relative superiority, and where they were largely unopposed by domestic producers. Toyota, Mitsubishi, Honda, and others followed and successfully established themselves. The fuel shortages and gasoline price spikes of the 1970s gave these small-car makers a huge boost and positioned them to move upstream into larger, more profitable segments. Figure 7-1 indicates how foreign producers, particularly from Asia, moved strategically from their initial beachheads into different market segments, mostly into the midrange. By the 1990s, some of these producers were introducing cars like the Lexus to challenge the high-end, profit-rich sedan segment; and they did the same in the fast-growing light-truck category.

Asian watchmakers followed a similar approach in the early 1970s when they entered the low end of the personal timekeeper market, where unit sales were potentially large but profits were small, and opposition from the dominant companies was weak. Precision watchmakers were unwilling to contest the Asian companies in those low-margin markets, but were content to retreat into the upper-end, high-profit segments of the market. Once the newcomers had established a beachhead, however, they developed products for those high-profit segments as well, forcing established European and North American producers to either compete more intensely or fold.

FIGURE 7-1

Moving beyond the beachhead

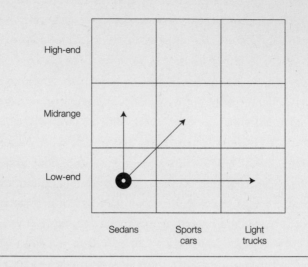

The lesson in both these examples is to follow Clausewitz's timeless advice of aiming the sharp end of the spear where rivals are weak or uninterested in what you're doing. That advice is applicable in just about every industry. Sam Walton, for example, did not initially go head-to-head with Sears or J.C. Penney, the retail giants of his day. Instead, he located his new Wal-Mart stores in small towns that were not served by those formidable rivals.

Think for a moment about the segments in your industry. Draw a map similar to figure 7-1. Which are the undefended segments where you could establish a beachhead? Once a beachhead is established, what would it take to expand into more profitable adjacent segments?

Market Entry Through Process Innovation

Some entry barriers cannot be outflanked as described above; they must be confronted directly. A direct confrontation with an established competitor is bound to be costly and dangerous. The better approach is to bring an innovation to the market—something that will turn the strengths of entrenched rivals into weaknesses.

Consider the example of the "mini-mill" first developed by Nucor Corporation, a newcomer to the industry, under the leadership of Ken Iverson in the 1980s. At the time, steelmaking was a mature business requiring huge capital assets and supply chains that stretched back to distant ore- and coal-producing operations. Sheet steel was produced through a batch process that poured mattress-sized slabs of white-hot metal and then gradually reduced slab thickness through a long and expensive series of rolling mills and reheating operations.

Nucor's innovation was to license a then-unproven German technology for continuous casting of thin metal slabs. This process needed very little milling or reheating. Nucor also opted to use scrap steel melted in electric furnaces as its raw material, eliminating the need for steel production from ore. Continuous casting had been an objective of steelmakers for almost a century, but until Nucor's bold gamble, no one had been able to make it work on a commercial level. In Nucor's hands, the innovation not only worked, but it ultimately cut the cost of steelmaking by more than 20 percent and provided Nucor with a successful market entry. Thanks to its innovative "mini-mills," the company has become the largest U.S. steel producer and is consistently profitable in an industry plagued by wide swings in customer demand. Its return on invested capital is a stunning 25 percent. "Big Steel," in contrast, discovered that its strengths—huge plants and labor forces, mining operations, and so forth—were now weaknesses.

Whether yours is a product or service company, process innovation may be your ticket to entering or gaining dominance in your target market. Have you or anyone else in your company given this approach any thought?

Market Entry Through Product Differentiation

Product differentiation is another strategy for gaining a market foothold. Inventor Edwin Land and the company he founded, Polaroid, did this in the photographic imaging business. During the 1950s, when Land was developing his technology, the photography business was already mature. Kodak dominated that business and many of its niches. Land would never make headway by producing his own brand of traditional films and cameras; that market was already well served. So he differentiated his product, creating a film capable of developing itself in one minute. This was new, this was different, and it set Polaroid apart. "Instant photography" was a big hit with many consumers, so much so that it allowed Land's company to flourish for decades until it was laid low by innovations in digital imaging.

To be successful, product differentiation must be valued by targeted customers. That's fairly obvious. But it must also be protected by patents or proprietary methods that make its duplication by rivals difficult or impossible. This is an aspect of differentiation that many overlook. George Eastman, founder of Kodak, hit the mother lode with his innovation of photographic film on a roll of cellulose. But Eastman went a step further. Understanding how easily his product could be duplicated by others, he protected it and the equipment he developed to manufacture it with an impenetrable thicket of patents. That protection helped his company stake out and dominate the photographic film business for generations.

Eastman's level of success is difficult to replicate. Most product differentiators are lucky if they can capture more than a two- or three-year monopoly. Consider the experience of Minnetonka Corporation, a small, Minnesota-based firm that introduced a product called "Softsoap" to a mature market dominated by huge national corporations. Softsoap came in a small plastic bottle with a handy pump. Liquid hand soap making isn't rocket science. Anyone with a small laboratory and rudimentary knowledge of chemistry can develop a marketable version of it. In fact, the first liquid soap developed in the United States received its patent in 1865. Over a century later, in 1980, Minnetonka introduced and branded its own version, which was a big hit. Any one of the big soap producer-distributors—companies that controlled shelf space in retail stores across the continent—could have introduced a rival version and smothered the upstart innovator under a tidal wave of promotion and store incentives. But Minnetonka had taken steps to protect itself in the short term by buying up the entire supply of plastic pumps needed for the liquid soap dispensers. That held the competition at bay for a while. Eventually, in 1987, Minnetonka Corporation sold its liquid soap business to Colgate-Palmolive, which has extended the brand with many product variations.

Create and Dominate a New Market

Are you struggling to match or outperform your rivals on cost, quality, or features? That might be a loser's game. A better approach might be to invent an entirely new market where no competitor has yet ventured. (See also "Breaking Free of the Old Formula.") And if you blanket key niches of that new market with good products or services, you will achieve a level of dominance that raises high entry barriers to others.

Breaking Free of the Old Formula

Success is often a barrier to market innovation because it enforces a formula that hamstrings innovation and change. For example, back in the late 1970s, the computing world was dominated by powerful mainframe computers, and IBM dominated that business. So, when personal computers began to appear, there wasn't a lot of interest within IBM. The people with organizational clout and big budgets were mainframers who understood how to make big computers and distribute them via corporate leases. Desktop computing and the selling of small, inexpensive machines to individuals were alien ideas within IBM. The only way the company could get its first PC into the market was through a *skunkworks* of engineers it set up in Boca Raton, Florida, far from the company's center of power.

Sometimes the best way to break free of the old formula and address a new market is through a new subsidiary or new operating unit that has been given substantial autonomy—and no rule book.

Consider Sony, which conceived of the personal portable stereo market and a product for tapping it: the Walkman. First introduced in 1979, the Walkman gave consumers great sound at a low price, in a small package that could be carried in a coat pocket or briefcase or attached to a jogger's waistband. No boom box could rival it for portability and sound quality. Millions of commuters, music buffs, joggers, and people stuck in office cubicles from nine to five bought them. To fill the many segments of this new market and thereby achieve dominance, Sony introduced different versions of the Walkman, almost all based on the same product platform: a more rugged sports version, one that included AM/FM radio, and so forth. And though rivals soon entered the market with versions of their own, Sony remained dominant and continued to introduce new models. It held that position until the advent of digital recording and playback devices.

What Sony accomplished decades ago has today been leapfrogged by the Apple iPod, a pocket-sized digital sound system capable of storing thousands of music files. These are fast becoming a must-have item for music lovers of all persuasions. Between its market launch in October 2001 and late 2004, consumers snapped up 5.7 million units.

Like Sony before it, Apple now offers iPod variants for different market segments, all based on the basic product platform (a form of incremental innovation). As of mid-2008, these included the iPod Shuffle, a 1- or 2-gigabite device capable of storing hundreds of files, the iPod Nano, a 4- or 8-gigabite unit with a 2-inch video screen, and the more powerful 2.5-inch-screen iPod Classic.

To create a new market, shift from building and making products to something more basic: satisfying customer's most pressing needs in new ways. Ask, "What could we offer customers if we forgot everything we know about our industry's current rules and traditions? How might we combine the advantages of several industries' offerings to provide new value for buyers?"

Throwing away the rulebook and starting with a clean slate isn't easy—especially if you've been successful under those rules—but it's the only way to think your way to new, competition-free markets.

Extending Innovation Through Platforms

The concept of product platform is another powerful strategy for extending innovation into the market. *A product platform*, as described by Marc Meyer and Al Lehnerd, whose work has largely defined this important concept, is "a set of subsystems and interfaces that form a common structure from which a stream of derivative products can be efficiently developed and produced."[2] In this strategy, the platform is the innovation; the rest is execution.

The ubiquitous Swatch watch is an example of a successful product family based on a common platform. The Swatch platform is a small set of timepiece subsystems linked together through a few electronic interfaces. This platform is, in effect, the innovation. Almost every Swatch uses the same platform, which is simple, inexpensive to manufacture, and capable of supporting endless external variations. This platform saved its maker, Société Micromécanique et Horologère (SMH), from business failure and helped it produce watches for fashion-oriented consumers with different tastes.

Product platforms based on design elegance and "manufacturability" give companies low-cost opportunities to customize their products for different market segments; figure 7-2 shows how the platform of common elements can be joined with some unique elements to produce a product (or service) for a particular market segment. Swatch did this by putting its innovative new clockworks inside a long series of uniquely designed band-case-face configurations, producing many "different" watches for different customer segments from a common base. The true innovation was in the clockworks. That innovation was leveraged in the marketplace by means of platform derivatives. Black & Decker did the same back in the early 1970s. In a classic case of platform innovation, Black & Decker very deliberately created a power tool platform—an electric motor and controls—on which it could base dozens of consumer power tools: electric drills, sanders, saws, grinders, and others. Thanks to that common platform and the cost advantage it conferred, Black & Decker was able to gain leadership in many consumer power tool markets. At the same time it was able to reduce

FIGURE 7-2

Addressing many market segments with a common platform

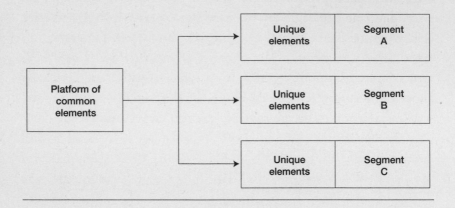

complexity in its operations. Instead of having to manufacture and stock unique motors, components, and switches for every one of its many power tools, the company could accomplish its goals using a single assembly program and common set of components. Costs and components were reduced by orders of magnitude.[3]

The SMH and Black & Decker examples are presented to underscore the value—in some cases—of focusing innovative thinking on platforms instead of on single products and services. What product or service platforms does your company use today? Are promising ideas conceived as single products/services or as platforms capable of supporting many different product/service families? If you are not using a platform approach, think of how a single platform could help you reduce costs, increase variety, and address different market segments.

This chapter has described a handful of practical strategies for moving an innovation to the marketplace. Perhaps one will apply to your situation. The total universe of these approaches is limited only by the human imagination. Be aware, however, that one's range of strategic possibilities is generally limited by practical constraints. For example, as described above, Sony and Apple successfully created new markets and filled key niches with imaginative products, but few business organizations have the creative talent, customer knowledge, financial capital, and technical wherewithal do the same or do so to the same extent. Likewise, a market-entry strategy based on a joint venture assumes that the instigator has something special to offer the venture partner. Not every firm has that.

So consider the strategic moves described here, but think also about your ability to adopt any one of them. What are the constraints on your ability to make a strategic move? What could be done to relax those constraints?

Summing Up

- Gaining and securing a market beachhead—even in a low-end or low-margin segment—can put you in a position to eventually expand into more attractive and profitable segments.

- When barriers to market entry are dauntingly high, avoid a costly direct assault. Instead, try to develop a new and superior process for doing what entrenched rivals are now doing.

- To be successful, product differentiation must be valued by targeted customers. To provide a defensible position, it must also be protected by patents or proprietary methods that make its duplication by rivals difficult or impossible.

- The strategic use of product or service platforms offers a cost-effective way of leveraging an innovation into different market segments.

- Acquisitions and joint ventures offer still other strategic moves for entering or expanding within a market. But beware—they often result in disappointment failure.

8

The S–Curve and Its Strategic Lessons

What Curve Are You On?

Key Topics Covered in This Chapter

- *The S-curve concept*

- *Lesson's from the S-curve for innovators*

- *Cautions in using the S-curve*

A S DESCRIBED IN chapters 1 and 2, incremental innovation that leverages or adapts a company's core technology is a safer and more predictable approach to keeping the cash registers ringing than is its radical counterpart. However, as the old saying goes, "every dog has his day," and many technologies eventually lose their competitive power and revenue-generating potency. Technologies (and services), like living things, produce cycles of growth and maturity; and as human needs change, or when new technologies emerge that satisfy need more effectively, those technologies enter a period of decline. This chapter uses the S-curve to describe these observations and to suggest how management can think about the life cycle of technology in strategic ways.

The S-Curve Explained

The course of successful technological innovation is often described through an S-shaped curve like the two shown in figure 8-1. An *S-curve* is plotted on a two-dimensional plane and demonstrates how the performance or cost characteristics of a technology change with time and continued investments. Here the horizontal axis reflects the unfolding history of technological innovations (investment over time), while the vertical axis indicates product/service performance or cost competitiveness.

The S-curve of the established technology is on the left in figure 8-1 and the curve of a newer rival technology is on the right. Notice

FIGURE 8-1

The S-curve: An established technology and a new rival

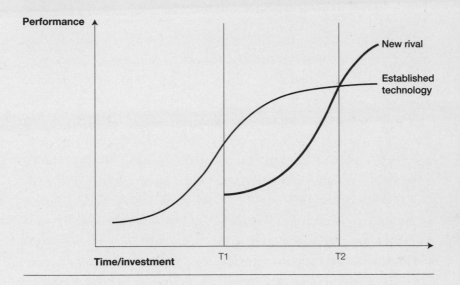

how the performance of the established technology has improved over time, at first rapidly and then at a modest pace. This is usually the result of investments and learning. Investments and learning by Hewlett-Packard, for example, have markedly reduced the costs and improved the performance of ink-jet printers over the years.

By the time the rival technology first enters the picture (T1), the established technology is already much improved and approaching its maturity. With maturity, the pace of improvement slows. Years of experimentation and incremental improvements have exhausted most of the opportunities to lower cost and improve performance. The proverbial "low-hanging fruit" has been picked. Every incremental gain in cost reduction and product performance is more and more difficult.

Now consider the S-curve of the new technology. Typically, the newly emerged rival technology is crude when compared with the established technology, with many issues yet unsolved—that's what we see at T1 in the figure. These weaknesses may cause established companies to write it off as "not a real threat." Most customers likewise ignore the new technology because it lacks the performance or cost characteristics they require—at least at the moment. The first-generation roll-film cameras developed by George Eastman late in the nineteenth century fit this description. The images produced by Eastman's roll film couldn't hold a candle to the superb images produced by chemically coated glass plates, the technological standard of that era, so the professionals and serious amateurs who constituted the photographic market in those days overwhelmingly rejected Eastman's photo film product. The same can be observed with respect to many of the innovative high-tech products introduced over the years. If you used the first-generation word-processing program for Apple's personal computer, you probably said, "I think that I'll hang onto my old typewriter." And with good reason. That early word processor had only uppercase letters, and the printers available at the time were expensive and produced low-quality output.

If the first-generation word processors were clunky, history tells us that the first typewriters were also unsatisfactory. Samuel Clemens (a.k.a. Mark Twain) was one of the first typewriter owners, and he complained often about its shortcomings. As he wrote to his literary friend, W. D. Howells, "*I dont know whether i am going to make this type-writing machine go or nto.*"

Many of the problems first associated with a new technology, however, are gradually solved. Manufacturing process improvements and scaled-up production cause costs to fall. The same often happens in the world of services; people work the bugs out of service innovations to the point of providing near-flawless delivery. Again, the performance/cost characteristics of the new technology improve with time and investment—typically slow in the beginning, but gaining speed thereafter. At a certain point (T2), the new technology matches its older rival in performance and/or cost features. But unlike the established technology, the new one has plenty of opportunities for continued improvement. If all goes well, it will improve to the point that its older rival will be displaced from the main marketplace.

This reversal of fortunes describes the observable plight of chemical-based photography today as it faces the challenge of digital imaging. Barring some technological breakthrough, the major opportunities for film improvement have been exploited. Those that remain will be costly and difficult to implement. Meanwhile, digital imaging can look forward to many years of improvements. It's already happening. The price of digital cameras keeps dropping, and performance gets better every year. It is very conceivable that film photography will survive only in a number of specialized niches, with digital imaging dominating all others.

The most dangerous period for a new technology is in the early phase, when its price-performance characteristics are below that of the established technology. If it can find and serve a niche market or lead users who, for one reason or another, value it, the technology may survive. If it can continue to improve its price-performance characteristics, it may even force its way into the mainstream market. The now-popular hybrid-powered vehicle provides an example.

The hybrid-powered cars first introduced by Honda and Toyota were revolutionary in concept—major departures from the century-old internal combustion-engine technology that dominates the existing auto fleet. When first introduced in 2000, these hybrid vehicles lacked some of the performance characteristics (acceleration and top speed) cherished by most drivers. But for the minority of motorists who really cared about fuel economy and the health of the ecosystem, traditional performance characteristics didn't matter. They were willing to takes a risk on this new technology and even pay a premium for it. As a result, hybrid cars found a niche and within just a few years were rapidly expanding into the mainstream. The fuel-cost crisis that struck like a lightning bolt in 2008 gave hybrids' market acceptance a huge boost. As the technology improves and as more drivers familiarize themselves with these new automobiles, it's likely that their sales will take a larger share of the broader market. This pattern is fairly typical of how successful innovations eventually displace established technologies and the companies that cling to them.

Successful innovations can also gain markets by following paths of diffusion:

- From military to civilian applications (e.g., GPS technology)

- From scientific to consumer uses (e.g., the Internet)

- From early adopter "techies" to lagging adopter non-technical users (e.g., personal computers)

It's worth noting, however, that older technologies do not always fade into the sunset as their challengers burst onto center stage. So we must approach this business of the S-curve with a certain amount of judgment and caution. The radio industry, after all, hasn't disappeared in the wake of television broadcasting; people still pack movie theaters, even though thousands of movie DVDs are available for less than half the price of a theater ticket; and millions of amateur astronomers still train their small telescope barrels skyward each night, despite the fact that immensely better images of planets and deep-sky objects are freely available on the Internet. In these and similar cases, the marketplace appears to have room for all.

Four Lessons

The scenario described by the two curves in figure 8-1 points to important lessons for business strategists. How can they migrate from the old, mature technology to the new? It is helpful to use the terminology of Richard Foster in describing companies associated with the established technology as "defenders" and adherents to the emerging technology as "attackers."[1]

Lesson #1: Defenders face difficult choices.

Companies that live off an established technology face difficult choices:

1. Abandon the business they already own, with all its cash flow and certainty, in favor of the rival technology, or

2. Hold onto what they have, and work hard to make it better or useful to more customers, or

3. Hold onto the existing business *and* begin investing in the new technology as a hedge against the future.

Of these options, the first (abandon the old) is the most difficult and is almost always impractical. How can any company afford to abruptly walk away from its current investments in skills and physical assets and still survive? When discount retailers emerged in the U.S. marketplace in the 1960s, for example, the big department stores like Sears, Filene's, and Marshall Field's, which dominated the market, could not abruptly follow suit: they had huge investments in properties, supplier relationships, and loyal customers. Only Minneapolis-based Dayton Hudson Corporation successfully made the transition to discount retail (Target).

Switching to an emerging technology usually requires new internal competencies and new facilities. The customer base may even be different and unfamiliar. Dropping everything to jump onto the new S-curve would be financial suicide in most cases. Also, commitment to the new S-curve is required exactly when doing so is most perilous—when the technology is still relatively crude and unsettled.

The second option—sticking to the current technology—is the easiest choice for decision makers. In the short run it produces no severe disruption. And it is quite possible that improvements to the current technology may extend its competitive life for a number of years. The nineteenth-century gas lighting industry managed to do this even as it developed new markets for its product (see "The Gas Industry Fights Back"). In the long run, however, sticking with an aging technology usually guarantees declining fortunes.

The third option—holding onto the existing business *and* investing in the new technology—is often the most practical course. The company can continue to operate the existing business and serve current customers as the new one develops. This is what Kodak has attempted as digital photography eats away at its existing film and photo-processing businesses. It is the choice that RCA, Sylvania, and others attempted decades earlier when their vacuum tube businesses were threatened by the appearance of solid-state transistors. The choice seems logical, but it has practical problems:

- The company may not have the competencies to develop the new technology. The film photography business, for example, is based on deep knowledge of chemicals, papers, mass production, and retail distribution; digital photography, in contrast, demands knowledge of advanced electronics and computing.

- The culture of the organization may not welcome the new technology. IBM ruled the world of mainframe computing and mainframe people ruled IBM. So when the decision was made in the 1980s to develop a PC business to serve the growing desktop computing market, that business was never treated seriously. The IBM PC had to be developed through a distant research lab. Later, IBM would go through a successful though wrenching migration from mainframes to e-business computing.

- Existing customers may pressure the company to stay in the old business. The discussion in chapter 2 of the "tyranny of served markets" pointed out that many, if not most, customers have a strong bias toward the established technology and will stick with it until the new one is demonstrably superior and less costly. Until that time these customers will urge companies to continue supplying them with parts and upgrades—in effect, telling them to stay in their old businesses.

In many cases, the best solution to these practical problems is for the established enterprise to develop the new technology within a separate subsidiary or operating unit.

Lesson #2: Leaders in one generation of technology are seldom leaders in the next.

Given the problems with each of the choices described above, it is not surprising that leaders of one generation of technology are seldom leaders of the next. The electronics business provides a fitting example. As described by Tushman and O'Reilly: "In the mid-1950s, vacuum tubes represented roughly a $700 million market. Leading firms . . . included such great technology companies as RCA, Sylvania, Raytheon, and Westinghouse. Yet from 1955 to 1982, there was almost a complete turnover in industry leadership, a remarkable shakeout brought on by the advent of the transistor."[2] The same

The Gas Industry Fights Back

As described by James Utterback in his engaging book, *Mastering the Dynamics of Innovation*, the many gas companies that produced and distributed illuminating gas for America's towns and cities enjoyed a comfortable monopoly until the 1880s, when incandescent electric lamps first appeared. Recognizing the threat, the gas companies fought back with incremental improvements to gas production and distribution. They also launched a public relations campaign that emphasized the dangers of electricity, and used their political influence to impede electric distribution. Those efforts, however, did little to hold back adoption of electric lighting.

The gas industry got a big break when Austrian inventor Carl von Welsback created a burner mantle that produced a fivefold improvement in gas lighting efficiency and a one-third reduction in operating costs. "This single improvement," writes Utterback, "threatened to sink the nascent electric light industry and explains why it took Edison twelve years to turn a profit in his fast-expanding electric lighting business."

Welsback's improvement gave gas lighting a momentary reprieve. But subsequent improvements were few and insignificant, leaving its cost/performance characteristics on a plateau. Meanwhile, electric lighting was making regular and substantial improvements in cost and performance, dooming gas as a form of lighting. The industry, however, survived and prospered by finding new markets in residential/commercial heating and process heat for industry.

SOURCE: James M. Utterback, *Mastering the Dynamics of Innovation* (Boston: Harvard Business School Press, 1994), 64–66.

phenomenon has been observed in many other industries. Here are a few examples:

- When mini-computers came along, upstart Digital Equipment became the leader, not IBM, the then-dominate computer company. When PC technology rose to the top, Digital missed the turn and lost its leadership to Dell, Hewlett-Packard, and other makers.

- Car rental companies around the globe had developed a finely tuned business model for providing auto transportation to customers for short periods of time—usually for one to seven days. They had the vehicles, multiple locations, and systems for making transactions. Zipcar created a new model for a very similar customer, urban dwellers who occasionally needed a car for an hour or a day. The innovative system it developed, which is now well entrenched in many U.S. cities and in the United Kingdom, caught the established car rental companies flat-footed. As of late 2008 they were still trying to figure out how to get into the short-term rental game.

- When eBay created its online auction site, traditional markets for used and collector items (classified newspaper ads, flea markets, and so forth) were never able to compete at the same level.

- As DVD videos became more popular in the United States, it wasn't the industry leaders (e.g., Blockbuster) that created a new business model for distributing them. An outsider, Netflix, stepped in with a better solution for most customers.

These examples may be disheartening if your company currently leads its industry. But while long-term decline is likely, it is not inevitable. Defenders, according to Richard Foster, can enlist various strategies to defeat upstart technological challengers:

- Leapfrog the attacker's technology: During the early stage of the S-curve, a new technology and its markets are undeveloped. If the attacker is a small company with limited resources, full development may be slow in coming. That leaves the large defender with greater resources an opportunity to jump onto the S-curve and capture the lead.

- Acquire the attacker: If the attacker's new technology appears poised to eat up your business, consider buying the attacker. If you follow this course, however, be sure to give the acquired company the autonomy it needs to succeed. Alternatively, consider licensing the attacker's technology.

Lesson #3: Attackers enjoy important advantages.

New technologies and innovative business models are often introduced through small, entrepreneurial firms. Industry powerhouses Virgin Atlantic, Hewlett-Packard, Intel, Apple, Microsoft, Amgen, Southwest Airlines, Dell, and eBay all began in this way.

Though entrepreneurial firms are generally weak in terms of brand recognition, manufacturing, and financing in their early stages, they often enjoy substantial advantages. Here are the most important:

- An undivided focus: Managers of upstart companies do not have to divide their attention between the ongoing business and the innovation because there is no ongoing business to speak of. Consequently, they can devote most of their attention to development of the new technology or business model.

- An ability to attract talent: Capable technical and managerial talent is often attracted to new ideas with promising futures, especially when stock options are a significant portion of compensation.

- Freedom from the influence of powerful customers: Many established companies fail to make the leap to the new technology because powerful customers persuade them to continue doing what they are doing. This is what happened to Goodyear Tire and Firestone when radial tire technology appeared. Not wanting to change their suspension designs, the Big Three U.S. automakers urged their suppliers to stick with bias ply tires. Michelin Tires, which had no supplier relationship with the Big Three, pressed forward, establishing leadership in the field.

- Little bureaucracy: Almost by definition, small entrepreneurial companies are unencumbered by the bureaucracy that burdens their larger rivals. That makes them fast and flexible.

- No need to protect investments in unrelated skills or assets: Established companies can find many reasons to not adopt new technologies or business models, such as:

  "We can't sell it through our existing distribution network."

  "It would cannibalize our current sales."

  "We just invested $50 million in facilities to manufacture our current product."

  "Our sales people wouldn't understand it; they'd have to be retrained."

- Entrepreneurial attackers do not have these concerns.

Lesson #4: Management should be alert to the next curve.

If you're a defender, take measures to know where an attack will come from. Are there nascent technologies on the horizon that, if perfected, would sink your business? Some companies use technology "scanners" to answer that question.

Limits to These Lessons

The S-curve is a useful thinking tool for managers. It describes generalized development paths for new and established products and technologies. But use it with this important caution: nothing about these paths is preordained; not every innovative technology overcomes its established rival. As Jay Paap and Ralph Katz have put it, "Success [with an existing technology] need not be paralyzing."[3] Indeed, we could probably fill a book with descriptions of innovative technologies that appeared promising but failed to make a sizeable inroad in the market. Gallium arsenide, for example, hasn't made a dent in the silicon-based chip business, as many had forecasted. Optical storage hasn't bested its entrenched magnetic rival as many predicted. And the list goes on. So look before you leap from one S-curve to another.

Nevertheless, management should always be alert for change and challengers. It must find the future and pursue it, the subject of chapter 9.

Summing Up

This chapter has explained the concept of the S-curve and its implications for managers and innovators. Here are the key points:

- An S-curve describes how the performance or cost characteristics of a technology change with time and continued investments. In the generalized model, a newly introduced technology is crude and not particularly competitive with established rivals, except in specialized niche markets.

- Performance and/or cost characteristics enjoy a period of rapid and steady improvement as technical issues are solved. Eventually, a new technology's performance or costs may eventually equal—and perhaps exceed—those of the established rival.

- A new technology does not stay new forever, but enters a period of maturity in which improvements are small, infrequent, and increasingly costly. At this point it becomes vulnerable to attack by still newer technologies that address problems or needs in different ways.

The S-curve concept was shown to have a number of lessons:

- Defenders face difficult choices with respect to how they should react to the appearance of a new technology.

- Leaders in one generation of technology are seldom leaders in the next.

- Attackers enjoy important advantages over established rivals: an undivided focus, an ability to attract talent, freedom from the "tyranny of service markets," little bureaucracy, and no need to protect investments in unrelated skills or assets.

To grasp the lessons of the S-curve, managers should:

- Stand back and contemplate where their companies and their key technologies are on the S-curve.

- Do the same for rival technologies, particularly those with promising futures.

- Determine which strategic option is most promising.

9

Finding the Future

Your Next Move

Key Topics Covered in This Chapter

- *Objective self-assessment of where one stands on the technology trajectory*

- *Alternative for firms in the mature or declining phase*

- *Signals of change and how to find them*

- *Where to put innovative projects that pursue the future*

CHAPTER 8 DESCRIBED the innovation S-curve and its often dire consequences for leading companies. As noted there, leaders in one generation of technology often fail to make a successful transition to the next wave of game-changing technology, and soon find themselves strategically out-flanked. Many of these former leaders ride their S-curves into decline and obsolescence. It's worth remembering that Sears, Goodyear, Xerox, Digital Equipment, RCA, U.S. Steel, and RCA once dominated their industries. All, however, failed to stay on top when technologies or markets experienced radical changes—in most cases, changes introduced or exploited by relative newcomers. Were the leaders of these companies brain-dead? Were they guilt of hubris—hapless victims of their own success? As Joseph Bower and Clayton Christensen have described it, the values and systems that make companies successful (and well managed) also make them unlikely to leap to the innovations in technology, service, or business model that will ultimately assure their fortunes:

> The research shows that most well-managed, established companies are consistently ahead of their industries in developing and commercializing new technologies—from incremental improvements to radically new approaches—as long as those technologies address the next-generation performance needs of their customers. However, these same companies are rarely in the forefront of commercializing new technologies that don't initially meet the needs of mainstream customers and appeal only to small or emerging markets.

Using the rational, analytical investment processes that most well-managed companies have developed, it is nearly impossible to build a cogent case for diverting resources from known customer needs in established markets to markets and customers that seem insignificant or do not yet exist. The processes and incentives that companies use to keep focused on their main customers work so well that they blind those companies to important new technologies in emerging markets.[1]

Given this grim observation, what can companies and their leaders do to dodge the bullet of change and get onto a new S-curve with future potential? This chapter attempts to answer that question. It involves scanning the current horizon of technologies, business models, and customer needs and trying to understanding where the future will lead.

Where Do You Stand Now?

The first thing one can do is to objectively assess the situation. The leadership team in concert with its brightest technologists (and, perhaps, informed third parties), should attempt to objectively assess the S-curve it's currently on, and the trajectory of that curve in the near and long term.

Return for just a moment to figure 8-1 in chapter 8. What is the current shape of your company's or unit's S-curve (labeled "established technology")? Is the slope of the curve currently rising rapidly with time and investment? Is there still room for substantial improvement to this technology? Are there many unexploited market opportunities to apply this technology? If there are, those are good reason to stick with it and keep investing in incremental improvements.

Is the slope of your S-curve at a point where every incremental improvement to its products, services, or technology is more and more costly to produce and less and less rewarding to you and your customers? If this describes your situation, you're in a dangerous place. Barring some breakthrough, the future of this technology may be stagnation and decline.

Now think about whatever new, rival technology poses a future challenge to your technology. Do you still enjoy performance/cost advantage over it? Is that advantage likely to last as the rival is perfected and its costs drop? If the answer is no, your company must change or face decline. You have several options:

- Embrace the rival technology—perhaps by acquiring the innovator company. As the saying goes, when faced with a steamrolling technology, you must either become part of that technology or part of the road.

- Leapfrog the rival technology with something better. In many cases, more than one nascent innovation is rising as a challenger; it's difficult to know which one will survive and flourish.

- Look for a breakthrough that will give your current technology a temporary new lease on life. For example, the hybrid power system being used by many auto manufacturers is an innovation that will extend the life of internal combustion auto engines for another decade or so before they totally succumb to other forms of propulsion (fuel cells, all-electric, etc.).

- Stick with the current technology, but find ways to leverage it into different markets. This is what the nineteenth-century gas lighting companies were forced to do as Edison's electric lighting technology was perfected and grew to dominate the market.[2]

Signals That Change Is in the Making

The fact that so many leading companies fail to identify and respond to emerging changes probably says less about the flaws of their leaders than about the inherent difficulty of spotting the new technologies, applications, and ideas that will truly reshape the future. With the benefit of hindsight, it's easy for us to ask, why did Western Union executives reject Alexander Graham Bell's offer to sell them telephone technology for $100,000, or why didn't Digital Equipment, the master of mini-computers, expand into personal comput-ing? Why was Dayton Hudson the only major department store company of many to catch the wave (with its Target stores) of dis-count retailing that now dominates the industry?

Unfortunately, the significance of changes like these is seldom obvious at the time. The new technology is usually weak and un-perfected and of little value to the majority of market customers, and its potential for improvement is unknown. Thus it's easy to ignore. In their book, *Seeing What's Next*, Clayton Christensen, Scott An-thony, and Erik Roth suggest that each of three customer groups may provide signals of impending change or the likely emergence of a new business model or technological change:

- Non-consumers

- Undershot customers

- Overshot customers

In their lexicon, under- and overshot customers refer to people or entities whose needs are not properly served. An example of an undershot customer would be a professional photographer who was offered a digital camera when those devices were initially made available to the public. Those early digitals lacked the image resolu-tion needed by the serious photographer. Improvements of various types would be needed to bring the product up to professional stan-dards. Table 9-1 is how Christensen and his coauthors describe these customers and the kinds of indicators that, as they say, "signal where change is possible, [and] where we can expect the future to be ma-terially different from the past."[3] In these situations, new products, services, and business models are likely to emerge.

The search for signals should also include old-fashioned scan-ning outside the company for signs of change. Some technology-oriented firms employ teams of forward scanners—scientists and engineers who make it part of their jobs to look outward toward the firm's markets, its competitors, and the world of technology. Their task is to look for anything that might threaten their current business or that could point out a direction they should follow.

TABLE 9-1

Overview of potential customer groups

Customer group	Identifier	What could happen	Signals
Nonconsumers	People who lack the ability, wealth, or access to conveniently and easily accomplish an important job for themselves; they typically hire someone to do the job for them or cobble together a less-than-adequate solution	New-market disruptive innovation	• Product/service that helps people do more conveniently what they are already trying to get done • Explosive *rate* of growth in new market or new context of use
Undershot customers	Consumers who consume a product but are frustrated with its limitations; they display willingness to pay more for enhancements along dimensions most important to them	Sustaining up-market innovation (radical and incremental)	• New, improved products and services introduced to existing customers • Integrated companies thrive; specialist companies struggle
Overshot customers	Customers who stop paying for further improvements in performance that historically had merited attractive price premiums	Low-end disruptive innovations Displacing innovation Downward migration of required skills	• New business model emerges to serve least-demanding customers • Emergence of specialist company targeting mainstream customers • Emergence of rules and standards—widely propagated statements of what causes what • Migration of provider closer to end customer

Source: Clayton M. Christensen, Scott D. Anthony and Erik A. Roth, *Seeing What's Next: Using Theories of Innovation to Predict Industry Change* (Boston: Harvard Business School Press, 2004), 5. Reproduced with permission.

As early as 1970, James R. Bright advocated something similar, which he simply called "monitoring." This method called for more than simplistic scanning and accumulation of data; instead, he advocated consideration of alternative possibilities from those observations and data. "The feasibility of monitoring," Bright wrote, "rests on the fact that it takes a long time for a technology to emerge from the minds of men into an economic reality with its resulting societal impacts."[4]

Create a Welcoming Home for the Future

Once you've identified an innovation with a promising future, the next question is, "Where will we put it?" Start-up firms that form around emerging technologies or unique services don't have a problem answering this question. Established companies with revenue-generating business lines are another story. They can either attempt to move the innovation project into an existing unit or allow it to work out of a skunk works or an autonomous unit. Many favor the latter approach. Clayton Christensen put it this way: "With few exceptions, the only instances in which mainstream firms have successfully addressed a disruptive technology were those in which the firm's managers set up an autonomous organization charged with building a new and independent business around the disruptive technology. Such organizations, free of the power and influence of the mainstream company's customers, can align themselves with a different set of customers—those who *want* the product of the disruptive technology."[5]

Lacking an autonomous organization, the business formed around the disruptive technology faces the danger of being killed, undermined, or sold by internal rivals and naysayers. The reason is easy to understand when one considers that the concerns of the established business and of the new business are poles apart. Worse, the new business will be evaluated by managers of the mainstream business, whose standards are profits and efficiency. The nascent technology offers neither. Also, the day-to-day concerns of these managers are diametrically opposed to those required by the innovative business, as shown in figure 9-1.

The new business fails to meet any of the standards of the mainstream business. So when the mainstream managers who run the place meet to discuss the future of the new business, it's not unusual for them to say, "This is draining investment funds from our profitable

FIGURE 9-1

What new and mainstream businesses worry about

Concerns of the new business	Concerns of the mainstream business
• Innovation	• Control
• Risk taking	• Predictability
• Market acceptance	• Operating efficiency
	• Profit margins

businesses. Let's pull the plug." Or, "It has potential, but not for us or our customers. Let's find a buyer."

As noted earlier, IBM attempted to avoid this problem when it first decided to produce a desktop computer, which entered the market in 1981. It set up a skunk works operation in Boca Raton, Florida, far from company headquarters, and gave its managers autonomy in designing and developing their product. GM did the same when it entered the small-car market in a serious way. It established Saturn as a separate operation, located it far from Detroit, and gave its managers a fairly blank slate on which to design their vehicle, production system, and labor-management relationship.

The danger, of course, is that these autonomous operations will be absorbed back into the parent organization as soon as they show signs of success—before they reach a point of self-sustaining development. Some observers believe that this was the fate of GM's Saturn operation.

Summing Up

This chapter offers suggestions for dealing with the grim possibilities suggested by the S-curve concept:

- The first of these was to think about where one stands on its current curve: are there still plenty of opportunities for cost and performance improvements in the existing business and its technologies, or has it entered a state of maturity or decline? An objective look at competitive or potentially competitive technologies is also in order. What is the likelihood of a nascent competitor making great strides in cost and performance? Answers to those questions should motivate action.

- Managers should also watch for signals that change is in the making. Those signals are often given by customers. They should also use scanning to pick up early indications of potentially threatening technological development.

- Equally important, organization leaders should create an environment in which innovative ideas are welcomed and not routinely killed off by managers who are absorbed by the operational concerns of the mainstream business: profitability, efficiency, and predictability.

10

Placing Strategic Bets

The Portfolio Approach

Key Topics Covered in This Chapter

- *Using the concept of portfolio management*

- *Mapping innovative projects by risk and return potential*

- *A method for quantifying project risk*

GOOD COMPANIES HAVE more ideas than they have resources to develop and exploit them. The concept of the idea funnel in chapter 5 was used to describe a process through which many ideas were winnowed down to the few on which the company will place its bets. That discussion did not, however, consider how innovative ideas can be handled in the context of company strategy and the risk-reward characteristics of individual projects and of those projects as a group.

Company strategy describes how an enterprise aims to differentiate itself in the marketplace. It's up to company leaders to articulate both a strategy and the areas within which they will entertain and support innovative ideas and projects. For example, leaders of a biotechnology company would probably want employees to innovate within specific areas (e.g., horticultural applications) and not others (e.g., human disease therapies). Doing so gives employees "boundaries" within which to direct their energies. The result is better-focused innovation and fewer wasted resources.

The risk and return characteristics of innovative ideas and projects presents another challenge for decision makers. Like a share of corporate stock, every project has a unique risk-return profile. Executives must consider an individual project's risk-return profile when they decide to commit or withhold support. This is typically addressed through portfolio management, which considers all projects under development.

Portfolio Management

Only the smallest firms deal with just one or two development projects. In contrast, big firms may have dozens of funded projects in play
at any given time. Some may be low-risk, short-term projects that
aim to incrementally improve an existing service; the reward potential of such projects is usually modest. Others may represent radically
new concepts that aim to create new markets; the reward potential of
these may be huge by comparison. Still others may fall between those
two extremes. Since incremental and radical projects entail substantial
differences in risk levels, time frames, and potential payoffs, management must employ portfolio thinking in dealing with them.

Portfolio thinking helps managers see a collection of ongoing
projects in terms of overall risk–return characteristics. And once they
understand those characteristics, they can shape and manage the
portfolio to achieve a balance of risk and potential return that suits
the aspirations of the company.

Portfolio management is a methodology widely used by both corporations and individual business divisions to create a proper mix of
new product/service or technology projects with the goal of:

- Maximizing portfolio value

- Diversifying risk

- Providing balance on many dimensions

- Supporting the strategy of the company or business unit

Portfolio management is the responsibility of the senior management team—often the same group that conducts stage-gate reviews. That team should meet regularly to manage the project
pipeline and make decisions about the project portfolio.

As a first step toward portfolio thinking, it is often helpful to
"map" ongoing projects onto a two-dimensional matrix like the one
in figure 10-1. Here, the horizontal axis indicates the potential payoff
of projects in the portfolio, as expressed by the expected net present

FIGURE 10-1

Innovation portfolio matrix

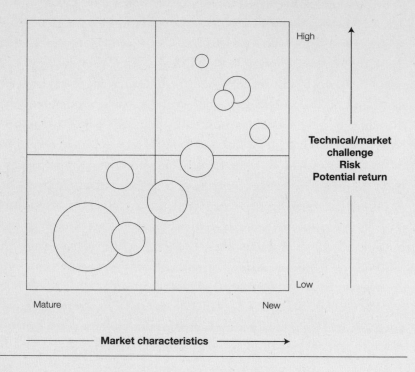

value (NPV). The vertical axis indicates rising levels of technical and/or market challenge, which are associated with greater uncertainty of success. Each circle in the matrix represents a project, and the size of each circle reflects the magnitude of resources dedicated to it.

In this matrix, the largest projects are cautious. In all likelihood, these address known markets and aim for incremental improvements. These projects are among the least technologically challenging and involve the least risk and least potential opportunity for the company. Several small projects populate the upper right quadrant. These may involve higher technological risk or new, unformed markets, but they also hold the prospect for greater economic payoff for the company if they succeed. The distribution of project numbers and project resources within the matrix reveals something about this company: It is fairly cautious, as indicated by the heavy weighting toward low-risk projects, perhaps with the goal of sustaining the existing business. However, it has placed several bets on high-risk, high-payoff projects. Does this represent the optimal balance for the company? Only senior management can answer that question. Only they can tell us if the portfolio is aligned with company strategy and whether it reflects the reality of the marketplace, the company's ability to take risks, and known technical factors (see "Best Practices in Portfolio Management").

Try constructing a similar matrix for your company. Once you've mapped out your current projects, what does the matrix tell you? If most projects and resources are located in the lower left quadrant, your company is being very risk-averse and may be doing

Best Practices in Portfolio Management

In a 1996 study involving hundreds of companies with substantial R&D budgets, Jim and David Matheson identified a number of best practices in R&D portfolio management, several of which are described here. The best companies, they found:

- Categorize, compare, and analyze the portfolio as a whole

- Balance truly innovative projects with incremental improvements

- Evaluate portfolio projects quantitatively

- Seek a proper balance across strategic objectives

- Address uncertainty in the language of probability

- Objectively discuss the implications of the success or failure of portfolio projects

- Hedge against technical uncertainty

SOURCE: David Matheson and Jim Matheson, *The Smart Organization: Creating Value Through Strategic R&D* (Boston: Harvard Business School Press, 1998), 70–74.

too little to address future opportunities, new technologies, and new markets. On the other hand, if most project and resources are in the upper right quadrant, it is being very aggressive. Ask yourself the following questions:

- What would constitute a suitable risk-reward balance for your company?

- What would be the optimal balance between projects that serve the existing business and those that aim to create new businesses?

- How many of your projects should be for the near term and how many for the long term?

- Who determines the portfolio's balance, and how are choices made?

No matter how they tilt the balance, all projects in a portfolio should be aligned with the strategy of the enterprise, and all should be subject to a common set of performance metrics: riskiness, return on investment (ROI), net present value (NPV), and internal rate of return (IRR) being the most widely used. Quality should be assured through periodic review of individual projects—and the portfolio as a whole—by a committee of decision makers and subject matter experts.

Getting a Handle on Risk

The matrix in figure 10-1 is widely used in managing portfolios of innovative projects and making decisions about where and to what degree a company should place its strategic bets. Research indicates that companies are betting more and more on low-risk, incremental innovation projects. According to Robert Cooper, the percentage of nonincremental innovation in company portfolios dropped from 20.4 percent to 11.5 percent between 1990 and 2004.[1] This may be due to the fact that in the risk-return trade-off the risks associated with radical innovation are more concrete and knowable than are their rewards, which are far, far in the future. Whatever the reason for this observable preference for incremental projects, it would be helpful if decision makers were better able to quantify the risk-return relationship in individual portfolio projects. Quantification would help them to more accurately place projects in the matrix.

Wharton professor George Day has provided a practical method for risk quantification. That method uses a matrix similar to the one shown in figure 10-1, but its x and y axes are defined more specifically and identify the probability of failure in each area (see figure 10-2). As he says, "estimates of the probability of failure have been thoroughly validated in dozens of interviews with consultants and senior managers involved in innovation initiatives and are consistent with recent surveys . . ."[2]

The position of a particular innovation project in this risk matrix is determined by answers to two questionnaires, shown in figure 10-3.

FIGURE 10-2

The risk matrix

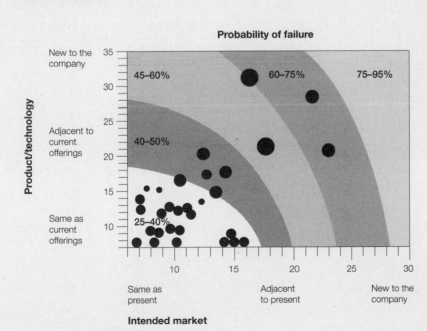

Source: George S. Day, "Is It Real? Can We Win? Is It Worth Doing: Managing Risk and Reward in an Innovation Portfolio, *Harvard Business Review*, December 2007.

FIGURE 10-3

The risk questionnaire

	Intended market					
	...be the same as in our present market		...partially overlap with our present market		...be entirely different from our present market or are unknown	
Customers' behavior and decision-making processes will...	1	2	3	4	5	
Our distribution and sales activities will...	1	2	3	4	5	
The competitive set (incumbants or potential entrants) will...	1	2	3	4	5	
	...highly relevant		...somewhat relevant		...not at all relevant	
Our brand promise is...	1	2	3	4	5	
Our current customer relationships are...	1	2	3	4	5	
Our knowledge of competitors' behaviors and intentions is...	1	2	3	4	5	
					Total (x-axis coodinate)	

	Product/technology					
	...is fully applicable		...will require significant adaptation		...is not applicable	
Our current development capability...	1	2	3	4	5	
Our technology competency...	1	2	3	4	5	
Our intellectual property protection...	1	2	3	4	5	
Our manufacturing and service delivery system...	1	2	3	4	5	
	...are identical to those of our current offerings		...overlap somewhat with those of our current offerings		...completely differ from those of our current offerings	
The required knowledge and science bases...	1	2	3	4	5	
The necessary product and service functions...	1	2	3	4	5	
The expected quality standards...	1	2	3	4	5	
					Total (y-axis coodinate)	

Source: George S. Day, "Is It Real? Can We Win? Is It Worth Doing: Managing Risk and Reward in an Innovation Portfolio," *Harvard Business Review*, December 2007.

The first concerns the intended market, an important source of risk: How similar is the innovation's intended market to the market currently addressed by the firm? The greater the similarity, the lower the risk, and vice versa. The "score" generated by this first questionnaire determines where a project stands on the x axis of the risk matrix. The second questionnaire considers the product (or service) and its underlying technology, another key component of risk: How familiar is the firm with the technology? The greater the familiarity, the lower the risk (on the y axis), and vice versa.

The two scores make it possible to locate a project on the matrix, thus providing two insights for senior management and innovation participants: (1) an estimate of each project's probability of failure (i.e., risk), and (2) a visual image of where—considering all innovation projects—the company is placing its strategic bets on the future. These insights can help management better judge whether it:

- Is too risk-averse or too daring

- Has too much focus on the immediate future or on the long term

- Has more projects than resources

Theoretically, this method could be applied to any innovation project—for products, services, process, or new technology. Can you think of opportunities where you could apply it today?

Bottom-Up or Top-Down Innovation?

As you place innovation bets, should you follow a top-down or bottom-up approach? Leaders of nations and enterprises alike have struggled with this question. At the national level, Japan's industrial policy identifies and supports R&D in areas deemed important to the country's future economy. That national strategy approach is heavily resisted in the United States, where few believe that the government is capable of picking winners. America looks to the creativity of entrepreneurs and corporations to pick winners and shape the country's future.

At the corporate level, we observe successful implementation of both strategies. GE, for example, places large bets on a limited number of what it calls "imagination breakthroughs"—projects with huge market potential. It looks to these major innovation projects to grow its business. And it has succeeded in this strategy to a substantial degree, thanks to breakthroughs in medical imaging, new-generation aircraft engines, hybrid-powered locomotives, and lighting, among others. Many point to Best Buy, the U.S. retailer of consumer electronics and home appliances, as a successful practitioner of the bottom-up strategy. Best Buy places it bets on many small experiments conducted at individual stores by employees of all ranks. These experiments aim to align store offerings with customer needs, reduce costs, and increase speed.

Which approach is superior probably depends on the nature of the innovations being sought. GE's strategic bets are on new, complex technologies that demand major funding. Best Buy's bottom-up innovations, on the other hand, are of a much lower technical nature and require little capital investment.[3]

Where does your company stand on the top-down versus bottom-up scale? Where should it ideally be?

Summing Up

This chapter has described the concept of portfolio management and how decision makers can use it to create a proper balance between innovation projects with different risk-return characteristics. The chapter also introduced a methodology for quantifying project risks resulting from the intended market and the underlying technology.

Project mapping on a two-dimensional matrix (expected reward versus uncertainty) helps decision makers see where they are placing their strategic bets, and how risk and return are balanced within the overall portfolio.

Portfolio management is supported by a number of best practices. These were enumerated in the text.

The chapter also provided a questionnaire-based tool for quantifying project risk. This tool asks managers to rate innovative ideas or projects in terms of (1) how similar or different they are relative to the market currently addressed by the company, and (2) how similar or different the technology is relative to those already familiar to the company.

Finally, the chapter addressed top-down and bottom-up innovation. It makes no judgment as to the superiority of either, but describes how they work and the capital investments attendant on each.

11

Human Creativity

The Starting Point of Innovation

Key Topics Covered in This Chapter

- *Creativity and the creative process*

- *Myths and realities*

- *The components of individual creativity: expertise, flexible and imaginative thinking, and motivation*

- *Managing for creative output*

EARLIER CHAPTERS OF this book focused on the front end of the innovative process: idea generation, opportunity recognition, and the processes that companies use to choose between many innovative ideas and move them toward commercialization. Very little was said, however, about the creativity from which ideas and innovations emerge, or about the things that managers can do to encourage it. We turn to these here and in chapter 12. But first, let's examine the concept of creativity and some popular misconceptions about it.

The English word *creativity* has its source in the Latin *creatus*, to have grown. It refers to the human act or process of producing a new idea or approach to a problem. Innovation follows in the train of a creative idea—that is, innovation is the process that applies the creative idea to development of a useful product, service, process, business model, or practice. Thus, creativity is the starting point of innovation.

What goes on in creativity? Many have tried over the decades to answer this question. Perhaps one of the most useful was formulated by Graham Wallas in his 1926 work, *The Art of Thought*, where creativity was described as a four-stage process of:

- **Preparation:** The individual's mind perceives the problem and explores its dimensions

- **Incubation:** The problem enters the unconscious mind (as many say, "I'm sleeping on it"). Synthesis of the bits and pieces of the problem no doubt occurs during this stage

- **Illumination:** The Aha! moment

- **Verification:** The stage in which the creativity idea is consciously verified, elaborated, and eventually applied[1]

Understanding the stages of this process will help you to better understand the creativity that is happening around you.

Myths About Creativity

Quite a bit of research has been done on creativity over the years. This research indicates misconceptions that limit the ability to effectively manage it. Five such misconceptions are described below.

Myth #1: The smarter you are, the more creative you are.

Reality: Intelligence correlates with creativity only to a point. Once you have enough intelligence to do your job, the correlation no longer holds. That is, above a fairly modest threshold—an IQ of about 120—there is no correlation between intelligence and creativity. As we will see later, there is no valid profile for the creative person; nor is there a test for determining a person's creative powers. So be careful about using IQ tests, grade point averages, and similar measures as you screen the people you look to for creative thinking.

Myth #2: The young are more creative than the old.

Reality: Age is not a clear predictor of creative potential. Research shows that it usually takes seven to ten years to build up deep expertise in a given field—the kind of expertise that enables a person to perceive patterns of order or meanings that are invisible to the novice. Thus, in the business world, the necessary creativity can be found in an adult of any age. At the same time, however, expertise can inhibit creativity: experts sometimes find it difficult to see or think outside established patterns. So when you think about staffing R&D or product development teams, think about creating a balance of veterans and newcomers. The veterans have deep expertise; the minds of newcomers are not contaminated by conventional thinking.

Myth #3: Creativity is for flamboyant risk takers.

Reality: A willingness to take calculated risks does play a role in creativity. After all, the innovator is stepping into unknown territory, expending resources that might have been directed to a less problematic venture, and possibly exposing his or her career to peril. But being creative doesn't mean you have to be a bungee jumper. It doesn't mean that you have to be markedly different from everyone else. Nor does it mean that creativity is restricted to high-risk endeavors.

Myth #4: Creativity is a solitary act.

Reality: Yes, a great many creative solutions are the product of a single person working in relative isolation. Isaac Newton, for example, developed his stunning theories on calculus, optics, and gravity during two years spent on his family's farm in rural Woolsthorpe (1665–1666), where he had sequestered himself to avoid an outbreak of the plague that had forced the closure of Cambridge University. Indeed, Newton's creative accomplishments during those two short years in the country may have been his most productive. Nevertheless, a high percentage of the world's most important inventions and technical breakthroughs are products of collaboration among groups of people with complementary skills. The Manhattan Project, which created the atomic bomb, and the Apollo Project, which put the first person on the moon, are just two examples of many. Thomas Edison, the most prolific inventor of his time, did not work alone but at the center of a large number of technicians, mechanics, and assistants—his famous "Insomnia Brigade," so named for their habit of working into the small hours of the morning.

Given the power of group creativity, smart managers look for ways to bring people with complementary skills and insights together: in forums, brown-bag lunches, workshops, skunk works, project teams, and brainstorming sessions.

Myth #5: You can't manage creativity.

Reality: Granted, you can never know in advance who will be involved in a creative act, what that act will be, or precisely when or how it will occur. Nevertheless, a manager can create the conditions that make creativity more likely to occur (rewards, resources, structures, etc.). Management *can* make a difference! This idea will be discussed in more detail later in the chapter.

Three Components of Individual Creativity

The myths we've listed cast doubt on the ability of managers to hire the right people and to create environments in which creative behavior can flourish. But these myths do not hold water. It's best to put them on the shelf and consider what creativity is, and the components that make it possible.

What is creativity? Robert Dennard described *creativity* as "the ability to produce or bring into existence something that was not there before, something new, an extension of our base of knowledge."[2] His experience in R&D convinced him that creative thinking was a process of posing important questions and finding answers. Albert Shapero, a management professor, has likewise identified creativity less as a trait than as a process—one that varies within individuals, but which nevertheless proceeds through identifiable steps of preparation, incubation, illumination, and verification.[3] Indeed, creativity is less about personal "wiring" than about a goal-oriented process of developing and expressing novel ideas for solving problems or satisfying needs. In many cases, this process allows a person to change his or her perceptions of reality, making it possible to "see" what most others do not.

Unfortunately, job candidates and employees don't wear lapel buttons that state "I'm creative." As Shapero has put it, "Despite several decades of research effort on creativity and highly creative individuals, there is as yet no profile or test that reliably predicts who will be highly creative in the future."[4] Although an individual's creative behavior cannot be predicted, the components from which creative behavior emerges have been identified. As described by Teresa Amabile, creativity has three components: expertise, creative thinking skills, and motivation (see figure 11-1).

Expertise

Expertise is technical, procedural, and intellectual knowledge—the know-how that often takes individuals years to accumulate. Expertise is usually the product of substantial preparation, a period of time

FIGURE 11-1

The three components of Creativity

Within every individual, creativity is a function of three components: expertise, creative thinking skills, and motivation. Can managers influence these components? The answer is an emphatic yes—for better or for worse—through workplace practices and conditions.

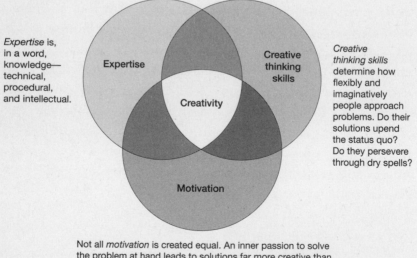

Expertise is, in a word, knowledge—technical, procedural, and intellectual.

Expertise

Creative thinking skills

Creativity

Motivation

Creative thinking skills determine how flexibly and imaginatively people approach problems. Do their solutions upend the status quo? Do they persevere through dry spells?

Not all *motivation* is created equal. An inner passion to solve the problem at hand leads to solutions far more creative than do external rewards, such as money. This component—called *intrinsic motivation*—is the one that can be most immediately influenced by the work environment.

Source: Teresa M. Amabile, "How to Kill Creativity," *Harvard Business Review*, September–October 1998, 77–87.

during which people look at problems or possibilities from many angles, "sleep" on them, experiment with them, develop a thorough understanding of the existing literature, and so forth. One advantage of creative teams over creative individuals is that teams can bring together the many forms of expertise needed to solve a large problem.

Creative Thinking Skills

Creative thinking skills are defined as how people approach problems. According to Amabile, creative thinking skills are often a function of personality and work style. "The pharmaceutical scientist," she writes, "will be more creative if her personality is such that she feels comfortable disagreeing with others."[5] It will also help if her work style is one that doggedly pursues solutions, even in the face of disappointing setbacks. The literature of invention is rich with stories of people who would not give up, but would stubbornly (almost obsessively) work at a problem despite repeated failures and the interference of higher-ups. Perhaps no better example can be found than the story of John Harrison, who labored almost forty years during the eighteenth century to develop a ship-borne clock capable of keeping accurate time despite rolling waves, dramatically shifting temperatures, and changing humidity. As told by science writer Dava Sobel in her best-seller, *Longitude*, Harrison had to fight through both technical challenges and countless roadblocks set up by competitors and naysayers in the scientific community of the day.[6] But his decades of dogged focus led to success and to a practical solution to a problem that had vexed mariners and scientists since ancient times: determining longitude at sea.

Motivation

Motivation may be extrinsic or intrinsic, according to Amabile. Extrinsic motivation is induced from the outside through means such as bonuses and promotions. Her research shows that intrinsic motivation—that is, motivation fired by an internal passion or interest—has a greater impact on creativity.[7]

The power of intrinsic motivation is confirmed by the many examples we see of engineers and scientists who continue to pursue solutions long after their bosses have cut off their funding (rewards) and told them to give it up and move on. Many of these creative spirits do this at substantial personal risk, going "underground" and supporting their work through clandestine resource channels.

A classic example of a motivated innovator can be found in the story of Dick Drew, the legendary 3M inventor of the 1920s and 1930s. Drew had seen a market opportunity for an adhesive-backed product that would later be known as "masking tape." After watching Drew's many failures to create the right combination of materials, his boss, 3M president William McKnight, told him to drop it and work on something else. Drew agreed, but secretly continued his quest, funding it with many small purchase orders that were within his authority to make but not likely to be noticed by McKnight. McKnight learned of Drew's insubordination only when the latter presented him with a successful product prototype. Drew's persistence paid off in a product line that has generated revenues for 3M for more than eighty years and is still going strong.

Managing for Greater Individual Creativity

Given what we know about individual creativity, what can managers do to get more of it? Clearly, creativity cannot be commanded. Nothing will be accomplished by telling employees that "The beatings will stop as soon as you become more creative."

One approach is to put a stop to the many ill-considered things that managers do that nip creativity in the bud:

- Punishing failure
- Encouraging complacency
- Withholding resources
- Making it difficult for people to share ideas
- Discouraging diversity of thinking
- Enforcing a convergence of viewpoints, or *groupthink*

You get the idea. Common sense tells us not to do these things. If these discourage creativity, opposite behaviors and policies should encourage it.

Amabile's three components—expertise, creative thinking skills, and motivation—likewise provide clues as to what managers can do to power up creative levels. These include:

- **Recruiting creative people:** Look for people who bring substantial expertise to the table and give others assignments and training that will increase their expertise.

- **Hiring people who have demonstrated the persistence and self-confidence that indicate creative thinking skills:** How can you spot a creative job applicant? One expert states that creative people are often intense. They look at a problem from many angles and take several approaches to finding a solution. Creative people, in his view, connect problems in one field with analogous problems in other fields.[8]

- **Getting the right match:** Matching the right people with the right assignments is highly motivational; it is the simplest and most effective approach to enhancing individual creativity. Effective matching is achieved when managers assign people to jobs that make the most of their expertise, their creative thinking skills, and their intrinsic motivations.

- **Giving freedom:** Amabile suggests that managers be specific about ends, but leave the means to their employees. Doing so will make them more creative. So instead of specifying a series of steps, say "This is our goal; think about the best way to get us there." Freedom, however, should not be absolute. Attaching reasonable deadlines and oversight is fair and part of a manager's responsibility.

- **Providing sufficient time and resources:** People are unlikely to be at their creative best when deadlines are arbitrary or impossible to meet. The same happens when people feel that they lack the resources to do the job well.

Tips for Increasing Your Own Creativity

If you are a manager, you need to help employees and groups be more creative. But what about you? What can you do to increase your own creativity? Here are eight recommendations:

1. **Strive for alignment:** Make sure that the goals of the organization you work for are consonant with your most cherished values. Instead of considering jobs at which you excel, think instead about jobs that match your deeply embedded life interests. Doing so will allow you to draw on a wellspring of personal passion.

2. **Imagine an ideal situation:** Sometimes simply envisioning an ideal situation will help you generate useful new ideas. For instance, if you were in charge of a service process that was slow, costly, and prone to errors, it might be useful to erase it from your mind and envision a situation in which you could deliver the same service faster, cheaper, and more reliably. Customers would be happy, and your company would save lots of money and frustration. Then ask yourself, "What could I do to create that ideal situation?" The answer might not come to you immediately, but if you assign the problem to your subconscious mind and return to it periodically, you may experience a creative breakthrough.

3. **Pursue some self-initiated activity:** Choose projects where your intrinsic motivation is high. If you have always loved graphic design, for example, try to determine why the packaging for one of your company's products leaves customers cold.

4. **Immerse yourself in the problem or challenge:** Instead of looking at a problem from the outside, dive into it. Experience the problem directly—for example, by assuming the position of a customer or user of an existing product or

service. Doing so will help you to understand the problem and possible creative solutions from many angles—many that you might not have anticipated.

5. **Tinker with the problem:** This will help you to better understand the problem and the strengths and weaknesses of the potential solution. For example, if you aimed to develop a faster sea kayak, you would learn a great deal by trying out existing models, experimenting with small-scale hull shapes, and so forth. As solutions present themselves, however, resist the temptation to grab onto any one of them prematurely.

6. **Be open to serendipity:** Develop a bias toward action and toward trying new ideas. For instance, if an accident or failure occurs while you're prototyping a new LCD screen, don't dismiss it too quickly. Study it for the learning opportunity that may lie within. Each day, write down what surprised you and how you surprised others.

7. **Diversify your stimuli:** Intellectual cross-pollination can get you thinking in new directions. Develop cross-functional skills: rotate into every job you are capable of doing. Get to know people who may spark your imagination. Become a lifelong learner: take classes not related to your work. Bring your insights from outside interests or activities to bear on your workplace challenges.

8. **Create opportunities for informal communication:** Take advantage of opportunities to exchange ideas and challenges with colleagues. One of them may have an insight that has eluded you. Creative thought often happens during spontaneous interactions between individuals. Such interactions, however, are only useful if real communication occurs. You must find ways to encourage and facilitate communication that is appropriate for the creative environment.

Summing Up

This chapter addressed the subject of creativity and individual creativity. It began with a practical definition and offered a four-stage process for how creativity works. This process includes preparation, incubation, illumination, and verification. It then exploded several myths about creativity. Contrary to conventional thinking:

- Intelligence and creativity are only weakly correlated.

- Age is not a clear predictor of creative potential.

- Calculated risk taking and the ability to think in untraditional ways play roles in creativity.

- A high percentage of important inventions are products of collaboration effect.

- Managers can make a difference in creativity output—they can create the conditions that make creativity more likely to occur.

Next, creativity was shown to have three components that you should bring to your organization's problems:

- *Expertise* in terms of technical, procedural, and intellectual knowledge;

- *Creative thinking skills*, as revealed by how people approach problems; and

- *Motivation*, both intrinsic and extrinsic.

Finally, the chapter identified practical things you can do to manage for greater individual creativity.

Individual creativity is always an important aspect of innovation. However, organizations accomplish most of their goals through teams or groups. What are the characteristics of creative groups? How can they be managed to greater productivity? These are the key issues addressed in the next chapter.

12

Working Through Creative Groups

The Power of Numbers

Key Topics Covered in This Chapter

- *Characteristics of creative groups*

- *Handling conflict in groups*

- *The effect of time pressure on creativity*

WHILE CREATIVITY IS sometimes an individual act, many innovations are products of creative groups. The transistor developed by scientists at Bell Labs is just one example. Groups can often achieve greater creative output than individuals working alone because they bring a greater sum of competencies, insights, and energy to the effort.

Characteristics of Creative Groups

In order to reap greater output, groups must have the right composition of thinking styles and technical skills. The "right" composition, in most cases, means a diversity of thinking styles and skills. Diversity has several benefits:

- Individual differences can produce a creative friction that sparks new ideas.

- Diversity of thought and perspective is a safeguard against *groupthink*—that is, the tendency of individual thought to converge for social reasons around a particular point of view to the exclusion of other views.

- Diversity of thought and skills provides opportunities for ideas to develop. An electrical engineer, for example, may seek a way to solve a technical problem while another engineer with manufacturing or materials experience may enhance the solution by suggesting ways that would make the end product less costly to produce.

Thus managers must consider how work groups are staffed and how they communicate.

A creative group exhibits paradoxical characteristics. It shows tendencies of thought and action that we'd assume to be mutually exclusive or contradictory. For example, to do its best work, a group needs deep knowledge of subjects relevant to the problem it's trying to solve, and a mastery of the processes involved. At the same time, however, the group needs fresh perspectives that are unencumbered by the prevailing wisdom or established ways of doing things. Often called a "beginner's mind," this is the perspective of a newcomer: a person who is curious, even playful, and willing to ask anything—no matter how naive the question may seem—because she doesn't know what she doesn't know. Thus, bringing together contradictory characteristics can catalyze new ideas. (See "Signs That Your Group Lacks Diversity" to help you evaluate your team.)

Figure 12-1 describes a number of seemingly contradictory characteristics that a group must have to maximize its creative potential. Many people mistakenly assume that creativity is a function

Signs That Your Group Lacks Diversity

If you're a manager, you'll know that your group lacks the diversity it needs to be its creative best if you observe one or more of the following:

- Members are reluctant to disagree with each other.

- The group has been working together for more than three years without infusions of new people.

- Members converge on plans and solutions very quickly and with little discussion.

- You suspect that minority opinions are not being heard.

- People regularly defer to a single person.

FIGURE 12-1

The paradoxical characteristics of creative groups

Beginner's mind	A team needs fresh, inexperienced perspectives as well as skilled expertise. Bringing in outsiders is often a useful way to provide the necessary balance of perspective.	Experience
Freedom	Your team must work within the confines of real business needs—and in alignment with your company's strategy. But it also needs latitude—some degree of freedom to determine *how* it will achieve the strategy and address the business needs.	Discipline
Play	Creativity thrives on playfulness, but business must be conducted professionally. Provide time and space for play, but clarify the appropriate times and places.	Professionalism
Improvisation	Plan your project carefully, but remember that projects do not always go as planned. When a researcher opens one door, he often finds several doors behind it. Encourage team members to look for ways to turn unexpected events into opportunities. Keep plans flexible enough to incorporate new or improved ideas.	Planning

Source: Harvard ManageMentor® on *Managing for Creativity and Innovation.* Adapted with permission.

of only the elements in the left column: the beginner's mind, freedom, play, and improvisation. But a blend of the left *and* the right columns is needed. This paradoxical combination is confusing and disturbing to managers who feel a need for order and linear activity. Accepting this paradox is the first step toward success.

Divergent and Convergent Thinking

Group creativity is also enhanced when both *divergent* and *convergent* thinking are at work. These terms were coined by psychologist J. P. Guilford, who conducted substantial research on creativity. In his lexicon, divergent thinking is the ability to find unique and original solutions and to consider problems in terms of multiple solutions—not just one. He viewed divergent thinking as a key component of creativity. Convergent thinking, on the other hand, narrows many possible solutions to one. In other words, thought patterns converge on a single, optimal solution.

The creative process is fueled by *divergent thinking*—a breaking away from familiar or established ways of seeing and doing. This seems intuitively obvious. If we continually observe an object from the same vantage point and in the same lighting conditions, we are bound to have the same impression of that object. If we change the lighting or the viewing angle, however, our perceptions may change. They will become more complete—more nuanced. For example, if you looked at the full moon through a small telescope, you would see a flat, bright, meteor-pocked surface with a modest number of striking terrain features. Look at it again a week or so later, when the moon's phase has created contrasts of sunlight and shadow, and you'll see something very different: rugged mountains, gaping crevices, and deep craters that were barely noticeable before. The different perspective created by light and darkness makes this possible.

Seeing things from unfamiliar perspectives makes it possible to develop insights and new ideas. But are those insights valuable? That's

Tips for Improving Convergent Thinking

Work groups are often tempted to converge quickly on what appears to be a single best solution and cut off future debate. It's the team leader or manager's job to prevent both. Consider these suggestions:

- Insist on an incubation period during which people can experiment with the various options. Some options will seem less promising after people have thought about them for a week or two.

- Appoint an official devil's advocate to challenge all assumptions associated with the group's favored options. That person should be respected and seen as objective.

- Ensure that dissent is tolerated and protected and that dissenters have the freedom to voice contrary views, otherwise groupthink may take control of future decisions.

what *convergent thinking* attempts to answer. It helps to channel the results of divergent thinking into concrete products and services. As new ideas generated by divergent thinking are communicated to others, they are evaluated to determine which ideas are genuinely novel and worth pursuing. That's convergent thinking. Without it, the creative person working alone could easily pursue an idea that eats up time and resources and leads to nothing of value.

In moving from divergent to convergent thinking, a work group makes a transition *from what is novel to what is useful*. Convergence sets limits, narrows the field of solutions within a set of constraints. How are those constraints determined? The culture, mission, and priorities of the company and project all contribute to the answer. They help rule out options that lie beyond the scope of the project.

Here are some questions your team might ask as it applies convergent thinking to a range of possible solutions:

- Which functions are essential (from the customer's point of view) and which are only "nice-to-have"?

- What criteria are determined by the company's values? For example, Fisher-Price groups insist that any toys developed be "Mom-friendly"—since most toys are purchased by mothers.

- What are the cost constraints?

- What are the size or shape constraints?

- Within what time must the project be completed?

- In what ways must the product or service be compatible with existing products or services?

Diverse Thinking Styles

Beyond divergent and convergent thinking, group creativity benefits when its members approach their work with different preferred thinking styles, and when they bring a variety of skills to a common effort. A *preferred thinking style* is the unconscious way a person looks at and interacts with the world. When faced with a problem or dilemma, a person will usually approach it through a preferred thought style. And although each style has particular advantages, no one style is better than another.

There are a number of different ways of describing how people think and make decisions. For example, the Myers-Briggs Type Indicator breaks down thinking preferences into four categories, with two opposite tendencies in each category:

1. **Extravert–Introvert:** Extraverted people look to others as the primary means of processing information. As they get ideas or grapple with problems, they quickly bring them to the attention of others for feedback. Extraverts energize themselves through their communications with others. Introverted people tend to process information internally first before presenting the results to others. They are happiest when they can sit down alone in a quiet place and think things through, weigh pros and cons, and so forth.

2. **Sensing–Intuitive:** Sensing people tend to prefer hard data, concrete facts—information that is closely tied to the five senses. Intuitive people are more comfortable with ideas and concepts, with the "big picture."

3. **Thinking–Feeling:** Thinking people prefer logical processes and orderly ways of approaching problems. Feeling people are more attuned to emotional cues; they are more likely to make decisions based on the values or relationships involved.

4. **Judging–Perceiving:** Judging people tend to prefer closure— they like having all the loose ends tied up. By contrast, perceiving people like things more open; they tend to be more comfortable with ambiguity and often want to collect still more data before reaching a decision.

Don't get hung up on the actual word used to describe any of these styles. Everyone exhibits some aspect of all eight, but they do it in varying degrees. For example, it's not that a feeling person is incapable of logical thought; rather, it's that his thinking about a decision tends to be more guided by the emotional impact of that decision on key relationships.

Well-balanced work groups include representatives of these different preferred thinking styles. How well-balanced are your work groups?

Diversity of Skills

Once you've assessed how the thinking styles of your group members complement (or duplicate) each other, you'll have a pretty good feel for whether any gaps exist. It is then time to survey the skills represented on the team. If the team lacks vital technical skills or expertise, it will have trouble developing the ideas it generates. For example, when Thomas Edison began thinking about producing the incandescent electric lamp, he knew that he would have to do lots of experimenting with designs and materials. So he created a team that included technicians with machining, laboratory, and glass-blowing skills. Their skills made it possible for Edison to test hundreds of filament materials in rapid succession. Eventually, a vacuum bulb containing a carbonized cotton filament proved serviceable. But more experiments with materials were needed before his idea could be commercialized. Again, the technical skill set he assembled made it possible to quickly perfect his "electric lamp" to the point where it would be commercialized.

In some cases, you may have to look outside your company—or industry—to find the technical know-how you need. For example, when engineers at a ceramics manufacturer experienced problems with getting ceramics to release from their molds, they realized that their problem had to do with quick-freezing—not with ceramics. So instead of seeking out other ceramics experts, they turned to food industry experts, who had special knowledge of quick-freezing.

Generally, you know that it's time to look outward for solutions when a group has been working for a long time on a problem without success. The same applies when team members always agree or always disagree on what should be done.

Tips for Filling Team Gaps

As you seek skills/knowledge diversification:

- Look for people whose intellectual perspectives comple-ment—but don't duplicate—your own preferred styles and skills, and those of your group.

- Look for a balance of expertise and personal characteristics (such as initiative, ability to get along with others, etc.) in each new hire.

- Look for people who can work across functional boundaries.

- When you specify hiring criteria, put a premium on finding the skills that the group currently lacks. Don't simply list a standard set of skills.

- Explore nontraditional hiring channels—that is, channels other than those used by your company's human resources department.

- Consider adding a customer or outside professional to the group. Either will bring a much different perspective. Xerox engineers, for example brought in anthropologists to help them design more user-friendly copiers.

Remember too that if your goal is to create change within the group, hiring one person who has a different perspective is insufficient. A lone hire with a different outlook many soon feel isolated and ineffective. For different thinking styles to make a difference, two things must happen: you must hire a critical mass of these people, and those people must be thoroughly integrated into the team.

Conflict in Groups—and How to Handle It

Although diversity of thinking and skills is valuable, it's not without hazards. Different thinking styles do not produce unbroken harmony—you would not want it in any case. Expect disagreement and clashes. The manager's job is to make conflict positive and creative.

For creative conflict to work, group members must listen to each other, be willing to understand different viewpoints, and question each other's assumptions. At the same time, managers must prevent that conflict from becoming personal or from going underground where resentment can simmer. The best antidote to destructive conflict is a set of group norms for dealing with it. What should your group's operating norms be? Here are a few examples. You might call them the "Group Code of Conduct."

- Every group member should show respect to others.

- Every member should make a commitment to active listening.

- Everyone has a right to disagree and an obligation to challenge others' assumptions.

- Everyone shall have an opportunity to speak.

- Conflicting views are an important source of learning.

- Ideas and assumptions may be attacked but individuals may not.

- Calculated risk taking is good.

- Failures should be acknowledged and examined for their lessons.

- Playful attitudes are welcomed.

- Successes will be celebrated as a group.

Whatever norms your group adopts, make sure that all members have a hand in creating them—and that everyone is willing to abide by them.

Three Steps for Handling Creative Conflict

Even with consensus on norms of behavior, conflict is a fact of life in groups. The following three steps will help you turn that conflict into a creative asset.

1. **Create a climate that makes people willing to discuss difficult issues:** Help your team understand the concept of "the moose on the table" (the big issue or problem that is impeding progress but which no one wants to discuss). Make it clear that you *want* the tough issues aired, and that *anyone* can point out a moose.

2. **Facilitate the discussion:** How do you deal with a moose once it has been identified? Use the following guidelines:

   • First, acknowledge the issue, even if only one person sees it.
   • Refer back to group norms on how people have agreed to treat each other.
   • Encourage the person who identified the moose to be specific.
   • Keep all discussion impersonal. The point is not to assign blame—discuss *what* is impeding progress, not *who*.

   If the issue involves someone's behavior, encourage the person who identified the problem to explain how the behavior affects him or her, rather than make assumptions about the motivation behind the behavior. For example, if someone is not completing work when promised, you might say, "When your work is not completed on time, the group is unable to meet deadlines," not, "I know you are not really excited about this product."

   If someone is not providing necessary leadership, you might say, "When you don't provide us with direction, we spend a lot of time trying to second-guess you, and that makes us unproductive," not, "You don't seem to have any idea what we should be doing on this project."

3. **Move toward closure by discussing what can be done:** Leave with some concrete suggestions for improvement, if not a solution to the problem.

If the subject is too sensitive and discussions are going nowhere, consider adjourning your meeting until a specified later date so that people can cool down. Or consider bringing in a facilitator.

Time Pressure and Group Creativity

Time is one of the things that every creative individual and creative group must have to achieve anything worthwhile. Radical innovations, as we've seen, often take ten or more years to emerge from the idea factories of research scientists. Incremental innovation of complex products such as new aircraft and new passenger cars often requires three to five years of development. Given these observations, how much time do creative people need? How much time should managers give them? These are important questions for managers as they attempt to meet organizational goals with limited resources.

Academics have studied the time pressure–creativity connection for a long time. In general, these studies point to a curvilinear relationship between the two—that is, to a certain point, pressure helps. But beyond that point, pressure has a negative impact. Teresa Amabile, Constance Hadley, and Steven Kramer continued that research, reaching some eye-opening conclusions. They point to instances where ingenuity flourishes under extreme time pressure—just as managers have always believed (or hoped!). They point, for example, to a NASA team that within hours came up with a crude but effective fix for the air filtration system aboard Apollo 13—a creative solution that saved the mission and its crew. On the other hand, they point to the Bell Labs teams that felt no such pressure; that team, nevertheless, created the transistor and the laser, which open the door to a cornucopia of innovative products.

After studying over nine thousand daily diary entries of people engaged in projects demanding high levels of creativity, Amabile and her coauthors concluded that time pressure usually kills creativity: "Our study indicates that the more time pressure people feel on a given day, the less likely they will be to think creatively."[1]

That's bad news for companies and managers, but not entirely bad. These researchers noted that time pressure affects creativity in different ways depending on whether the environment allows people to focus on their work, conveys a sense of meaningful urgency about their tasks, or stimulates or undermines creativity in other ways. For example, time pressure is not a creativity killer when people feel that they *are on a mission*, which is what the NASA crew undoubtedly felt.

To help managers understand when and how time pressure affects creativity, we've shown the four-quadrant matrix developed by Amabile and her associates in figure 12-2.

Finding the Right Balance in Group Tenure

If your job is to manage a team or work group that aims to innovate, one of the many things you should pay attention to is the length of time that group members have worked together, or group tenure. Years of working together doesn't always produce the creativity you'd expect. Beyond a certain point, the opposite is more likely. In this regard, work groups are similar to organizations and products, which have life cycles stages. Those stages are generally associated with one level of vitality or another. Consider the typical product life cycle shown in figure 12-3. Here we see what usually happens with a successful product. Upon introduction it picks up steam on the sales front (the growth stage). Eventually, growth tapers off (the maturity stage), and at some point sales go into decline. Research by Ralph Katz and Tom Allen indicates that R&D groups pass through a similar set of stages if no actions are taken to prevent it. As Katz described their findings: "[G]roup members interacting over a long time are likely to develop standard work patterns that are both familiar and comfortable, patterns in which routine and precedent play relatively large parts— perhaps at the expense of unbiased thought and new ideas."[2]

Katz and Allen found that individuals who enter these groups pass through stages of varying innovation productivity. On entering an R&D group, individuals first undergo a period of *socialization*,

FIGURE 12-2

The time pressure/creativity matrix

Our study suggests that time pressure affects creativity in different ways depending on whether the environment allows people to focus on their work, conveys a sense of meaningful urgency about the tasks at hand, or stimulates or undermines creative thinking in other ways.

	Time pressure	
	Low	High
High	Creative thinking under low time pressure is more likely when people feel as if they are *on an expedition*. They: • Show creative thinking that is more oriented toward generating or exploring ideas than identifying problems • Tend to collaborate with one person rather than with a group	Creative thinking under extreme time pressure is more likely when people feel as if they are *on a mission*. They: • Can focus on one activity for a significant part of the day because they are undisturbed or protected • Believe that they are doing important work and report feeling positively challenged by and involved in the work • Show creative thinking that is equally oriented toward identifying problems and generating or exploring ideas
Likelihood of creative thinking **Low**	Creative thinking under low time pressure is unlikely when people feel as if they are *on autopilot*. They: • Receive little encouragement from senior management to be creative • Tend to have more meetings and discussions with groups rather than with individuals • Engage in less collaborative work overall	Creative thinking under extreme time pressure is unlikely when people feel as if they are *on a treadmill*. They: • Feel distracted • Experience a highly fragmented workday, with many different activities. • Don't get the sense that the work they are doing is important • Feel more pressed for time than when they are "on a mission" even though they work the same number of hours • Tend to have more meetings and discussions with groups rather than with individuals • Experience lots of last-minute changes in their plans and schedules

Source: Teresa M. Amabile, Constance N. Hadley, and Steven J. Kramer, "Creativity Under the Gun," *Harvard Business Review,* August 2002, 56.

FIGURE 12-3

Typical product life cycle

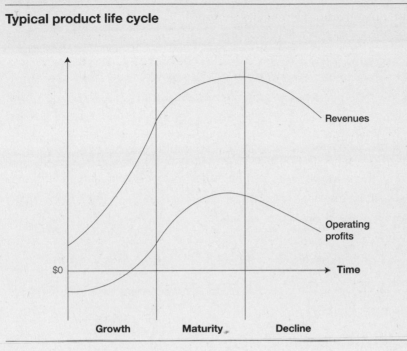

during which they spend as much time trying to understand group norms, their bosses' expectations, and so forth as they spend on innovative work.

The socialization stage is followed by an *innovation* period during which they are generally most productive. Individuals in this stage understand the norms of the group and where they fit in, and can concentrate on creative, innovative pursuits. After a while, however, individual group members enter a less-productive period of *stabilization*. As Katz says, "Employees who continue to work in the same overall job situation for long periods gradually adapt to such steadfast employment by becoming increasingly indifferent to the challenging aspects of their assignments." Like most other corporate employees, these stabilized R&D workers are less absorbed with the challenges of their work and more absorbed with matters of compensation, benefits, vacations, workplace relationships, and issues with their superiors. "With stability," Katz writes, "comes a greater loyalty to precedent, to the established patterns of behavior. . . employees become increasingly content with customary ways of doing things" and so forth.[3] Further study indicated that tenure in the group, not chronological age, had the greatest influence on creative productivity.

What solution is available to managers? Ideally, they should try to keep people in the productive *innovative* period, but how can that be done? Periodically rotating people into other assignments, a commonplace refresher practice, may not be a good solution, as it puts the employee back into the relatively unproductive socialization period. The solution, according to Katz, lies with group managers and how they supervise. He found that managers of high-performing long-tenured groups were:

- Highly respected for their technical accomplishments

- Were *not* practitioners of participative management, but were more directive

- Set demanding goals

- Challenged people to work in new ways

- Had strong bases of support with senior management

Does your group have this type of leadership?

Summing Up

This chapter addressed the subject of creativity in individual and teams. Organizations have found that innovation is generally a function of collaboration between individuals working within groups. With that in mind, the chapter identified the characteristics of creative groups. Groups must have the right composition of thinking styles and technical skills. The "right" composition, in most cases, means a diversity of thinking styles and skills. It also means bring together some paradoxical characteristics:

- The "beginner's mind" and experience

- Freedom and discipline

- Pay and professionalism

- Improvisation and planning

Group creativity is also enhanced when both divergent and convergent thinking are at work:

- Divergent thinking is a breaking away from familiar or established ways.

- Convergent thinking attempts to find the value of creative insights.

The chapter also examined the issue of time pressure, which affects both individual and group creativity. Is time pressure a good thing or bad thing? Much research has been done on this issue, and the latest indicates that pressure affects creativity in different ways, depending on whether the environment allows people to focus on their work, conveys a sense of meaningful urgency about their tasks, or stimulates or undermines creativity in other ways.

Finally, the chapter noted the importance of work group tenure, and how you can keep a group from getting stale. The answer, according to two authors, was determined by management style.

13

Toward a Creativity– Friendly Workplace

Practical Steps

Key Topics Covered in This Chapter

- *Six ways to organizational enrichment*

- *How to enrich the physical workplace*

H IRING CREATIVE PEOPLE and posting them into well-crafted teams and work groups, as described in chapter 12, are essential steps toward producing greater creativity and innovation. The next step is more difficult and requires support at the highest levels. It involves making the organization and the workplace more supportive of creativity and innovation. Just as seeds grow best in fertile soil, the natural creativity of people is more likely to blossom within an organization whose structures, attitudes, and policies are innovation-friendly.

Even if you have put together a really hot team of creative people, that team will produce disappointing results if it's condemned to operate within an organization that's unfriendly to new ideas. This was precisely what people in Xerox Corporation's Palo Alto Research Center (PARC) experienced during the late 1970s and early 1980s. PARC was (and remains) a cornucopia of innovative thinking. Its scientists and engineers had conjured up many of the technologies that would eventually power the emerging era of desktop computing: the ethernet, the mouse, and a user-friendly operating system. Xerox management, however, was not receptive to those innovations, which were not going to produce financial returns in the time frame required by the company. Many of PARC's innovations found their way into personal computers developed by Apple.

Hewlett-Packard innovators encountered a different but equally frustrating experience around 1990. The open, decentralized organization created by founders William Hewlett and David Packard had been highly encouraging to innovators and had put the company at the forefront of many emerging product categories. But the retirement of the founders, new management, and enormous business growth resulted in a more centralized and bureaucratic organization. People with innovative ideas found that they had to gain approval from many layers of committees before they could move them forward. The result was a marked slowdown in new product introductions and plummeting profits. Thankfully, the company's aging founders intervened, broke up the bureaucratic tangle, and returned HP to its idea-friendly ways. A huge leap in new product introductions followed—as did profits.

The Xerox and Hewlett-Packard examples underscore the impact of organizational practices on creativity and the innovations it produces. Table 13-1 lists the characteristics that support and encourage creativity and innovation. Consider these characteristics and how your company or your operating unit stands relative to them. Is it strong? Is it weak? If it's weak, what can be done to change the situation? This chapter considers each characteristic in detail.

TABLE 13-1

Does your organization embody the characteristics that support creativity and innovation?

	Strong	Weak
Risk-taking is acceptable to management		
New ideas and new ways of doing things are welcome		
Employees have access to knowledge sources: customers, benchmarking partners, the scientific community, and so forth		
Good ideas find supportive executive patrons		
Innovators are rewarded		
Physical surroundings bring people together		

Risk Taking Is Acceptable to Management

Risk aversion is normal and healthy. But progress and risk are insep-
arable companions. You cannot have one without the other. "You
have to promote risk taking," Esther Dyson told readers of *Harvard
Business Review.* "Be open to experimentation and philosophical
about things that go wrong. My motto is, 'Always make a new mistake.' There's no shame in making a mistake. But then learn from it
and don't make the same one again. Everything I've learned, I've
learned by making mistakes."[1]

Management must recognize the risk/reward relationship and
find organizational mechanisms for handling it. And it must communicate a clear understanding that reasonable risks are acceptable,
since they are the companions of progress. On the innovative front,
two methods are available for dealing with risk: diversification and
cheap failures. These can and should be used in concert.

Diversification allows companies to spread risk over many rolls
of the dice—as was made clear in the earlier chapter on portfolio
management. For example, if one hundred individuals are taking
calculated risks on innovative ideas, experience will generally show
that some will be total failures, others will roughly break even, and
some others will be very successful, producing a net positive outcome for the combined one hundred ventures. Since one can never
know in advance which ideas will be the winners and which the los-
ers, having a diversified "portfolio" of ideas in play makes sense.

Cheap failure is the second method for dealing with risk. A
cheap failure is a project or experiment that is terminated with the
least outlay of resources—just enough to tell managers "This isn't
going to work." We find a direct analogy to cheap failure in card-
playing. A smart cardplayer knows that he can't expect to win if he
stays out of the game. So he puts down his *ante* and waits for his
cards. If those cards are strong, he'll stay in the game, matching or
raising other bids. As he draws more cards, the player will decide
whether staying in a particular game is worth the cost, given the
odds. His goal is to get out of losing games as cheaply as possible.

Smart companies treat ideas in the same way. They back promising ideas with small budgets and look for ways to test them with the least resource inputs. Like cardplayers, they quickly fold when they recognize that they have a weak or losing hand. Conversely, they increase backing for strong ideas.

New Ideas and New Ways of Doing Things Are Welcome

The worst environment for creativity is one that is unwelcoming to new ideas. "Why bother to come up with new ideas," people ask "when management shoots down everything?" Some senior managers are, in fact, so bound up with the status quo that they have little enthusiasm for anything that's new or different. "We've been successful over the years by doing things this way, so why should we change?" An organization with this attitude is heading for trouble.

In fairness, management is compelled to shoot down good ideas when (1) those ideas lack a strategic fit with the business, or (2) the organization lacks the resources to pursue them. In these cases, however, management has a responsibility to communicate its reasoning to employees.

Beyond welcoming new ideas, the organization should view innovation as a normal part of business—not a special activity practiced by a handful of employees. That's the advice of Craig Wynett, general manager of future growth initiatives at Procter & Gamble. "What we've done to encourage innovation is make it ordinary," says Wynett:

> By that I mean we don't separate it from the rest of our business. Many companies make innovation front-page news, and all that special attention has a paradoxical effect. By serving it up as something exotic, you isolate it from what's normal . . . At P&G, we think of creativity not as a mysterious gift of the talented few but as the everyday task of making nonobvious connections—bringing together things that don't normally go together. . .

Isolating innovation from mainstream business can produce a dangerous cultural side effect: creativity and leadership can be perceived as opposites. This artificial disconnect means that innovators often lack the visibility and clout to compete for the resources necessary for success.[2]

People Communicate Freely

Open communication is another characteristic of an innovation-friendly organization. Communication and information sharing often catalyze idea generation and development within groups. Here's why. Many creative ideas are formed *at the intersection of different lines of thought or technology.* For example, Harold is working on vehicle steering systems; Maude is an expert in electromechanical applications. When these two communicate and share information, they may get an idea for an electronic steering system that hasn't yet been considered.

In hierarchical firms, information is hoarded as a source of organizational power. Information flows are controlled and channeled through the chain of command, and people must demonstrate a "need to know" to have access to certain information. This control impedes the catalytic function of communication and limits opportunities for different pieces of information to intersect and combine in peoples' minds. For example, if Harold and Maude are not able to communicate directly with one another, their new steering system idea may never germinate.

Managers can encourage the free flow of information in many ways: through e-mail, the physical co-location of team members, joint work-sessions, and regular brown-bag lunches. They can also strengthen the unseen but critically important communication networks that link people together and act as information conduits. Managers should ask:

- Who are the "go to" people on key issues?

- Who is communicating with whom?

- What physical or location barriers are preventing frequent and effective communication between people who should be in regular contact? Would "co-location" of particular people improve communication and results?

- Are our R&D people isolated from contacts with sales people, market researchers, and customers?

An effective communication network is often one of the greatest facilitators of creativity and invention. Experienced managers recognize this and do what is necessary to remove impediments to communication between people.[3] People need to see and interact with other team members on a regular basis. When this is accomplished, small pieces of information that by themselves mean nothing may be joined together to create important insights. This is best accomplished when they are situated in close physical proximity. Videoconferencing and e-mail are poor substitutes for physical co-location and the cohesion that normally develops through frequent and direct contact. Consider the use of a "team room" dedicated to team activities (see "The Team Room Concept").

The Team Room Concept

A *team room* is a dedicated physical space within which full- or part-time members of a work team can congregate to do their work, share information, brainstorm, and so forth. It serves as a central "node" in the communication network that holds participants together and facilitates the information and idea sharing that so often leads to breakthrough insights.

As described by Marc Meyer and Al Lehnerd, a team room can also serve as a repository for physical and informational artifacts that help stimulate creative thinking: market research reports, prototypes, disassembled competing products, white boards and flip charts, timelines, and so forth.[a]

a. For more on team rooms and their use, see Marc H. Meyer and Alvin P. Lehnerd, *The Power of Product Platforms: Building Value and Cost Leadership* (New York: Free Press, 1997), 138–139.

Knowledge Is Shared

Just as employees must have free-flowing lines of communication between one another, they also need access to sources of knowledge—both inside and outside the organization. That knowledge is often the raw material of creative thought.

Some companies have developed elaborate knowledge-management systems to capture knowledge, store it, and make it easily available for re-use. These systems help assure that what was learned by someone in Unit A doesn't have to be learned anew by someone in Unit B. Lee Sage has described the Engineering Books of Knowledge (EBOKs) used by a major U.S. manufacturer, a knowledge management database containing technical data, lessons learned, and best practices that is made available to the company's engineering community. The purpose of the EBOKs, according to Sage, is to capture the expert knowledge of technical employees and use it to improve engineering productivity, speed new product development, and to avoid repeating past mistakes.[4] Consulting and tax accounting companies use knowledge management systems in similar ways.

Another way to help employees tap sources of internal knowledge is through the creation of communities of interest. A *community of interest* is an informal group whose members share an interest in some technology or application. The group many be a dozen engineers from different operating units who share a common interest in adhesive applications. It might be a group of managers interested in service process improvement. Whatever the interest may be, newsletters and periodic meetings held by these communities provide opportunities to share knowledge and spark the imagination.

External knowledge is equally important as a stimulant to creativity and innovation. External knowledge invigorates and adds vitality to organizations. Employees tap that knowledge when they have opportunities to attend professional and scientific meetings and to visit customers and when outside experts are brought in to share their know-how via lectures and workshops.

One of the classic cases of tapping external sources of knowledge occurred in the early 1980s when Xerox Corporation sent a team of logistics personnel to visit the warehouse of outdoor outfitter L.L. Bean. Xerox had identified "picking, packing, and shipping" of individual replacement parts and user supplies as a critical bottleneck in its fulfillment operation. To eliminate that bottleneck, it began searching for best practice know-how. Library research turned up an article identifying L.L. Bean as a company that had mastered the art of quickly and accurately filling small, individual orders of one to three items—just what Xerox was attempting to do without success. Within a short time, a Xerox team was dispatched to Freeport, Maine, to observe L.L. Bean's methods, which were later adapted successfully to the copier company's fulfillment process.[5]

What sources of external knowledge are your people tapping today? Do they have resources and management encouragement to seek out relevant knowledge?

Good Ideas Find Supportive Executive Patrons

Organizations need people in high places who will champion good ideas and provide them with moral support and protection as they travel the bumpy road toward commercialization. Richard Leifer and his colleagues observed a form of executive patronage in each of the radical innovation projects they studied. They concluded, for example, that IBM's silicon-germanium computer chip project would likely not have survived without the implicit protection of two senior IBM executives, who over a period of years provided under-the-table resources to keep that project alive. They observed the same at GE, where a now-successful digital X-ray technology would have died on the vine had it not been for the backing of two high-placed executives—one being then-CEO Jack Welch.[6]

If you had a great idea, would anyone in senior management have the interest and the courage to act as its patron? Would that person provide protection and resources? Would he or she connect you to people who could help?

While executive patronage is often necessary for radical innovation, its support is not always well directed. Senior executives are not necessarily more clairvoyant than other managers, and they sometimes place their bets on the wrong horses. Motorola's Bill Galvin backed the costly Iridium misadventure. Polaroid's Edwin Land invested heavily in Polarvision, a failed attempt to produce instant movies. And Steve Jobs, who demonstrated great foresight in other areas, lost heavily in his support of NEXT. Nevertheless, research points to executive patronage as an important contributor to radical innovation.

Innovators Are Rewarded

Creativity will not flourish in the absence of a reward system that encourages individuals to stretch beyond the bounds of normal work. Creative energy dissipates and must be somehow replenished. Rewards serve this purpose. They can be based on:

- **Recognition:** Acknowledging individual or group achievement with a plaque or public announcement

- **Control:** Allowing an individual or group to participate in decision-making or giving them the resources they need to carry out a project

- **Celebration:** For example, acknowledging a successful new-product launch by throwing a party

- **Rejuvenation:** Providing time off to attend a technical conference.

Rewards can either be intrinsic or extrinsic. An *intrinsic reward* appeals to a person's desire for self-actualization, curiosity, enjoyment, or interest in the work itself. An *extrinsic reward* appeals to a person's desire for attainment distinct from the work itself: a cash bonus, a promotion, or stock options. These two sources of motivation work hand in hand. Especially when the work is not routine, intrinsic motivation can help generate creative thought. Just make sure that the rewards or incentives you establish don't become more important than the work itself, thereby undermining team members' intrinsic motivation. But at the same time, don't underestimate the power of money, recognition, or other incentives to bolster a group member's self-esteem, and thus enhance his intrinsic motivation.

If you are managing a creative group, it's highly unlikely that you'll have the authority to create a compensation plan for your team, but you may have the power to tweak the existing system of informal rewards to better suit your team's situation.

The Physical Surroundings Bring People Together

As we've seen, organizational features—culture, if you will—have an effect on the creative output of managers and employees. If the organizational environment doesn't expect, encourage, or honor creativity, it will get exactly what it anticipates—very little. In contrast, organizations that have been wellsprings of creativity over many decades—companies such as 3M, Ciba-Geigy, Corning, Siemens, Hewlett-Packard, Apple, Motorola, Nokia, Procter & Gamble, and others—organize and behave as through creativity matters.

Physical surroundings can also have an impact on creativity. Even though space costs are usually second only to people costs, many executives are just awaking to the importance of place. Like the organizational environment, the physical environment can be engineered in ways that encourage higher creative output. For example, when an environment is filled with many types of stimuli, and when it provides physical and electronic links between individuals, it encourages people to see new connections and to think more broadly.

In the late 1990s, a team of researchers at MIT's School of Architecture and Planning—the Space Organization Research Group (SORG)—began looking at the connection between workspace design and work processes. They found that, in general, companies attempt to fit work processes to a fairly standard set of physical surroundings—the warren of office cubicles and conference rooms that most of us inhabit from 9 to 5. They allow work processes to be determined by existing spaces, which are essentially fixed. This is like putting the cart before the horse. Work processes need the flexibility to alter themselves from time to time as objectives vary.

One of SORG's more interesting case studies involved a workspace being developed for a new project team at a Xerox research center in New York state.[7] There, the space and the work were designed simultaneously and with a high level of coordination. Team members were co-located for easier communication with each other and with the physical equipment that occupied their thoughts and experiments. Lines of movement into, out of, and through the workspace were deliberately laid out to create opportunities for frequent and convenient contact between teammates. Meeting rooms were designed so that physical artifacts in the labs were in sight and physically accessible. Meetings were open to all.

Though the actual outcome of the Xerox case could not be determined during the period of SORG's observation, a small but growing body of research is demonstrating what intuition would tell us—that workspace design and work effectiveness are linked.

Modern management's shift toward less formal, team-based ways of working has forced architects and designers to develop spaces that are more adaptable to work process changes and more supportive of creative and cognitive patterns of work. This is the logic behind BMW's Munich engineering center, the *Forschungs- und Innovationszentrum*, or FIZ.

The building, which opened in1987, is based on the concept of co-location. Its ninety thousand square meters of floor space bring together in one site everyone concerned with auto product development, including BMW's suppliers. Approximately five thousand researchers, engineers, and technicians work in the FIZ, which is designed around a network that links various groups together. The maximum walking distance between any two FIZ occupants is 150 meters. That encourages physical contact and informal communication between the many people who work toward common objectives.

What's the nature of your workplace? Do you work out of a closed office where contacts with other key people are strictly accidental or planned in advance?

Tips for Improving the Physical Environment

You may not be able to design your workspace from the ground up, but there are valuable—and relatively inexpensive—steps you can take to enhance your team's physical surroundings. The idea is to encourage the interactions that lead to information sharing and creative ideas.

- Conversations and spontaneous meetings often occur in public areas: in mailrooms, in coffee-rooms, and around water coolers. So make these spaces into comfortable gathering places where people will linger and share ideas.

- Place comfortable chairs in alcoves to create casual meeting areas.

- Place whiteboards and flip charts in places where people naturally congregate. This will allow them to sketch out their ideas during a spontaneous discussion.

- Spread crayons and white paper on conference and lunch-room tables to encourage doodling and idea diagramming—two modes of thought that are very different from verbal discussion.

- Institute a weekly brown-bag lunch at which people take turns telling their coworkers about their ideas and soliciting feedback.

- Give teams "war rooms" in which they can meet, plan, post information, and display competing products.

What is the physical distance between you and the people with whom you should be interacting and sharing ideas on a regular basis? Organizational researchers have known for a long time that the frequency of communication between co-workers decreases dramatically as the physical distance between them increases. As MIT researcher Tom Allen discovered years ago, "People are more likely to communicate with those who are located nearest to them. Individuals and groups can therefore be positioned in ways that will either promote or inhibit communication."[8] Thus workspace design and the physical location of project team members has a major impact on the depth of communication and knowledge sharing. Use worksheet 13-1 to think about ways your own organization can use space to foster innovation.

How Friendly to Creativity Is Your Workplace?

As this chapter makes clear, creativity is a function of many things, including how it is managed. For a diagnostic checklist that you can use to evaluate the creativity of your workplace, see appendix B.

The 3M Way

Many of the practices recommended here for creating an innovation-friendly organization and culture can be observed in one of American's oldest enterprises: Minnesota-based 3M Corporation. 3M has evolved from a maker of sandpaper to a manufacturer of hundreds of different products, including adhesives, films, and fiber optics. In more than a century, it has commercialized over fifty thousand products, many of which have generated revenue streams lasting many decades. Its success as a long-term innovator is generally attributed to its corporate culture, which very deliberately fosters creativity by giving employees the freedom to take risks and tinker with new ideas. That culture is a legacy of William L. McKnight (1887–1978).

McKnight joined 3M in 1907 as an assistant bookkeeper, but rose through the ranks, becoming president in 1929 and board chairman in 1949. During his tenure he worked to create a culture that put employees in direct contact with customer problems, which encouraged initiative and innovation. His philosophy was to listen to anyone who

WORKSHEET 13-1

Enhancing the creativity of the physical workspace

The physical environment can help or hinder creativity and innovation. Use this worksheet to inventory your workspace and generate ideas for improvements that take into account possible alterations.

Dimension	Current condition	Ideas for improvement
Accessible, casual meeting space		
Physical stimuli (for example, books, videos, art on walls, journals)		
Space for quiet reflection		
Variety of communication tools (for example, whiteboards, bulletin boards, e-mail)		
Employee-only space		
Customer contact space		
Space for individual expression		
Game or relaxation area		

proposed an original idea, and to let that person run with the idea through "experimental doodling." As he wrote in 1948:

> *As our business grows, it becomes increasingly necessary to delegate responsibility and to encourage men and women to exercise their initiative. This requires considerable tolerance. Those men and women to whom we delegate authority and responsibility, if they are good people, are going to want to do their jobs in their own way.*
>
> *Mistakes will be made. But if a person is essentially right, the mistakes he or she makes are not as serious in the long run as the mistakes management will make if it undertakes to tell those in authority exactly how they must do their jobs. Management that is destructively critical when mistakes are made kills initiative. And it's essential that we have many people with initiative if we are to continue to grow.*[9]

Today the company backs up McKnight's management philosophy with a number of creativity-supporting practices. Here are just a few:

- McKnight's notion of experimental doodling is institutionalized into 3M's unofficial "15 Percent Rule," which allows technical and scientific employees to use that percentage of their time to pursue ideas unrelated to their official assignments. The 15 Percent Rule has spawned a number of commercially successful products over the years.

- The work of outstanding technical employees is recognized by admission to the prestigious Carlton Society, which opens its doors to a few remarkable innovators each year. These individuals are chosen by their peers in recognition of their contributions to 3M technologies and products.

- Teams that create products that earn $4 million or more in profitable revenues receive the Golden Step award.

- Employees can choose between management and technical career ladders. Not everyone is cut out to be a manager, and not all who are qualified for management want to leave the laboratory. Providing a career direction choice, and rewarding each, gives people a chance to make their greatest contributions.

These organizational features are part of 3M's culture of innovation, and they help account for its success in producing new and useful products decade after decade. That culture is changing with new management and a new competitive environment, so there is no guarantee that it will remain a culture of innovation.

Summing Up

This chapter focused on the factors that promote or stifle creativity. The first of these were organizational:

- A sensible level of risk taking is accepted.

- New ideas and ways of doing things are welcome.

- Information flows freely.

- Employees have access to knowledge sources, including customers.

- Good ideas find support among executives.

- Innovators are rewarded.

But the organization isn't everything. The physical workplace can also inhibit or enhance creativity. Drawing on several lines of research, the following practices were suggested:

- Co-locate teams and knowledge sources for easier communication.

- Design the physical space so that contact between teammates is frequent and convenient.

Leaders Can
Make a Difference

It's in Their Hands

Key Topics Covered in This Chapter

- *Fixing the culture so that it nurtures creativity and innovation*

- *The importance of communicating strategic boundaries*

- *Seeking innovation in unusual functions*

- *Leader behaviors that support innovation: being active in the process; being open but skeptical; putting the right people in charge*

- *Improving the idea-to-commercialization process*

- *Overlooked areas of innovation*

JUST ABOUT EVERYTHING that gets done in a sizable company with respect to innovation is accomplished by rank-and-file employees: marketing and sales people who see new opportunities; technical professionals and engineers who formulate novel solutions; middle managers who facilitate idea sharing and brainstorming. But senior leadership also has a major role to play: it alone has power to shape the culture, establish the boundaries of innovation efforts, allocate resources, and create a balance between today's concerns and those of the future. This chapter offers practical suggestions for what leaders can do to strengthen the innovative efforts of their organizations.

Fixing the Culture

The impact of organizational culture on creativity and idea generation was discussed in several chapters of this book. In the absence of a supportive culture, creativity and innovation are like seedlings planted in arid, rocky soil. They simply won't germinate and grow without it.

Michael Tushman and Charles O'Reilly point to pre-Louis Gerstner IBM as a culture in which innovation fell on poor soil. It was, in their words, "a culture characterized by an inward focus, extensive procedures for resolving issue through consensus and 'push back,' arrogance bred by previous success, and a sense of entitlement on the part of some employees that guaranteed jobs without a quid pro quo."[1] If those words describe your company's culture, then creativity and innovation are not likely to flourish. And the most innovative people will become discouraged and dispirited. The antidote is cultural change, which is a job for senior leaders. Those leaders should ask themselves:

- Is our current success making us self-satisfied and complacent?

- Are we inwardly focused?

- Do we punish risk takers who fail?

- Are creative people and new ideas unwelcome in this company?

- Are we excessively bureaucratic in how we handle new ideas?

- Do we fail to reward acts of creativity?

If you answered yes to any one of these questions, a serious change in organizational culture may be in order. Unfortunately, cultural change is probably the most difficult type of change. Top management and a small team of consultants can change the structure of an organization by fiat through reorganization, merger, or divestiture. Change that involves downsizing can also be commanded from the top. But to change an organization's culture, people must be motivated and induced to think and act differently. That's a major shift that takes time and the support of people at every level. It cannot be commanded.

A major crisis—even a near-death experience—is often a prerequisite of successful change. British Airways, Continental Airlines, and IBM each experienced crises in the 1990s, and in each case a combination of immediate peril and strong leadership provided the motivation that employees needed to support cultural change.

This raises an important question: "Do we have to wait for a crisis before change is possible?" No, according to Harvard Business School professor Michael Beer. He believes that change leaders can create legitimate concerns about the current situation, and offers these four approaches for doing so:

- **Use information about the organization's competitive situation to generate discussion with employees about current and prospective problems:** Top management, Beer says, often fails to understand why employees are not as concerned about innovation, customer service, or costs as they are. Too often this is because management has failed to put employees in touch with the data. In the absence of that data, everything appears to be fine.

- **Create dialogue on the data:** Providing data is one thing. Creating dialogue on the data is something entirely different. Dialogue should aim for a joint understanding of company problems. Dialogue is a means by which both managers and employees can inform each other of their assumptions and their diagnoses.

- **Create opportunities for employees to educate management about the dissatisfactions and problems they experience:** In some cases, top management is out of touch with the weaknesses of the business or with emerging threats—things that frontline employees understand through daily experience on the factory floor or in face-to-face dealings with customers. If this is your company's problem, find ways to improve communications between top management and frontline people.

- **Set high standards and expect people to meet them:** The act of stating high standards creates dissatisfaction with the current level of performance.[2]

Establish Strategic Direction

Setting strategic direction is another responsibility of senior leaders. If creative people don't understand where the company is headed, they are likely to generate and pursue ideas that don't fit with current capabilities, that eat up resources, and that will eventually be rejected prior to commercialization. That costs money and dissipates energy.

Since both creative energy and money are usually scarce, it makes sense to encourage idea generation within boundaries defined by company strategy. For example, if you're a direct-mail apparel merchandiser, you may wish to encourage ideas that fall within the boundaries of "forming better linkages with our customers and providing fast and accurate order fulfillment." Within those strategy-related boundaries,

Tips for Changing Organizational Culture

1. **Make sure that all four change-ready conditions are present:**

   - Leaders are respected, credible, and effective.
   - People are dissatisfied with the status quo and feel personally motivated to change.
   - The organization is nonhierarchical.
   - People are accustomed to and value collaborative work.

   Changing the culture of an organization in the absence of these four conditions is extremely difficult. So if your company lacks any one condition, work on it first.

2. **Mobilize energy and commitment to change through joint diagnosis of business problems:** Remember, you can't order energy, commitment, and innovation the way you would a monthly report; but you can generate them if you involve people in the process of identifying problems and solutions. In most cases, they will know more about the problems and opportunities than you will since they are closer to them.

3. **Don't try to change everything at once:** Unless the entire organization is in crisis, begin with change-ready units far from corporate headquarters, where local managers and their people can run the show and maintain control. Use successful change in those units as test beds from which to spread change gradually to other units.

4. **Create an appealing and shared vision of the future:** People won't buy into the pain and effort of change unless they can see a future state that is tangibly better—and better for them—than the one they have at the moment. Successful change leaders form such a vision and communicate it in compelling terms.

Continued

> 5. **Support change from the top, but leave the thinking and doing to unit leaders and those most affected by the change:** Above all, don't put human resource personnel in charge. Give the responsibility to unit line managers.
>
> 6. **Celebrate milestones:** Cultural change is a long journey with many milestones. Celebrating the achievement of each milestone recognizes progress and reenergizes commitment.

new ideas for improving customer intelligence, order processing, and logistics would be welcomed. Set the boundaries right and your company's creative energies will naturally focus in areas with the greatest payoff potential.

The effect of setting strategic direction and establishing boundaries for ideas will be much greater if you do three things:

1. **Communicate:** This might seem obvious, but it's rare to find an organization whose employees can clearly articulate company strategy—particularly employees at lower levels. "I just do my job," they'll say. So communicate strategic direction clearly and often.

2. **Hire right:** Make employee selection and recruitment a critical issue, not a distraction. Use every hiring opportunity to populate the organization with people whose special training, experience, or personal interests and passions are aligned with the strategic direction of the company.

3. **Align resources with strategy:** People follow the money. Once they see ideas that fall within stated boundaries being funded for development, they'll channel their creative energies in that direction. Senior management should also review its existing development projects and pull the plug on those that no longer enjoy a strategic fit.

Be Involved with Innovation

Some of the best and most successful executives are happiest and most effective when they were down in the R&D lab rubbing elbows with bench scientists and technicians. Bill Hewlett, David Packard, Bill Gates, and Motorola's Bob Galvin fit that description. It's impossible to make a direct correlation between the R&D involvement of these executives and the success of their organizations, but we know intuitively that leaders cannot make good decisions if they operate in a vacuum or think of innovation as a mysterious force. They must understand the technical issues facing their organizations and the portfolio of ideas and projects that are in the pipeline at any given time. Hewlett, Packard, Galvin, and Gates all did this.

Most corporate leaders do not or cannot keep their connection with the innovation side of their business—and they pay a price. In a speech given to the Industrial Research Institute in 2003, former GE executive Lewis Edelheit reflected on the problem that senior managers have when they are pulled away from R&D work and immersed in the business side of the enterprise. "It is impossible," he said, "if you are in the middle of a business to see what's happening from the outside." [3]

More importantly, leaders must assess the individual innovators who drop new ideas into their laps from time to time. Because they are enmeshed in the world of the business, and less in the world of technology and customers, they must ask questions like:

- Who are these idea people anyway?

- Do they have good judgment?

- Do they understand customers and the way customers see the world?

- Are they cautious optimists or hucksters who'll give me all the reasons to say yes but conceal every reason for saying no?

These questions cannot be answered if decision makers and innovators operate in orbits that never intersect. The best way to answer these questions and provide leadership for innovation is to be personally involved. So visit the research center on a regular basis. Have lunch with project teams. Get to know key people one-on-one. Try to understand the technical hurdles that stand between appealing ideas and commercialization.

Research by Harvard Business School professors Kim Clark and Steven Wheelwright indicates that few senior leaders follow that advice. Their involvement in development projects typically begins when projects are nearing the end of the development process: in the pilot or manufacturing ramp up stages. This is too late in the game to affect the shape or direction of projects, and reduces the role of senior leadership to "kill" or "go."[4]

Organizational leaders should do just the opposite. They should be visible and personally involved in the early stages of the innovation process. Doing so has four important benefits:

1. It sends a powerful signal to employees that innovation matters.

2. It provides senior management with opportunities to articulate the strategic direction of the firm and the boundaries within which innovation should be pursued.

3. It gives senior management a direct hand in the design of products and services that will define the company in the future.

4. It educates leaders on technical and market issues and prepares them to act as recognizers and patrons of good ideas.

So if you are a senior manager, ask yourself these questions:

- Am I spending only a very small percentage of my time on the innovation front?

- Am I leaving early design decisions to low-level personnel who may not understand the big picture of our business?

- Have I become insulated from the technological issues shaping our business?

- Is my involvement so late in the innovation development process that my only interest is in whether a project will clear financial hurdles?

If you answered yes to any one of these questions, reconsider how you're spending your time. Innovation and R&D are the crucibles within which the future of your company is being formed today—you need to be there.

Be Open but Skeptical

Close contact with innovation and R&D will test your judgment. Some people will "pitch" their ideas to you and look for support and resources. Approach these encounters with a balance of open-mindedness and scientific skepticism. That means two things: (1) demonstrating an interest in new ideas, even when they challenge the company's current products and ways of operating; and, (2) simultaneously maintaining scientific skepticism. The two are not incompatible; they can be achieved through honest dialogue, as in this example:

I think that this new service would really sell.

Leader: *Really? To whom?*

Well, to our current customers and to others.

Leader: *Why do you believe that? What problem would the service solve for them?*

It would save them lots of time.

Leader: *How much time would it actually save them? And how much would they be willing to pay for that benefit?*

I can't answer either of those questions yet.

Leader: *Then give some thought to how we can find the answers, and let's talk again.*

Notice how the leader in this example demonstrated an interest in the idea by suggesting a course of action but reserved judgment until the uncertainties are reduced. Responsibility for reducing those uncertainties was placed on the shoulders of the idea generator. If you use a stage-gate system, each gate provides an opportunity to test the validity of ideas and projects in this way. As a leader, you should participate in that system at the most strategic and critical points. In most cases, those will be the initial gates, where the idea's fit with strategic direction is generally determined.

Improve the Idea-to-Commercialization Process

Earlier chapters in this book described an innovation process that begins with idea generation, and then proceeds though various stages that evaluate and develop worthy ideas into commercialized products and services. Like every process, the innovation process should be continually scrutinized for improvement opportunities. Make sure that your process:

- Generates a sufficient number of good ideas; if it's not generating enough good ideas, find the cause and fix it

- Is free of bottlenecks that impede promising ideas and frustrate innovators

- Is free of politics

- Encourages calculated risk taking, but isn't afraid of killing off bad ideas

- Is nonarbitrary

- Creates cheap failures

- Channels resources and the brightest people to the most worthy projects

- Involves people who understand the company's capabilities, its strategy, and its customers

Like culture change, improving the innovation process is a job for senior management. And it's one of the most important jobs they will ever handle.

Tips for Senior Management

- Keep friends and yes-men off the board. You need unvarnished advice as you consider investing in innovative ideas.

- Surround yourself with people who have complementary skills and different approaches to analyzing issues and making decisions. Listen to their suggestions and arguments, even if you disagree. These other voices will help you to avoid walking off a cliff.

- Learn when to cut your losses. To win any game you must participate. But don't play every game to the end. Recognize when you're pouring resources down a dry hole, and have the fortitude to bail out when you do.

- Always double-check your assumptions. What looks rosy can be a disaster if those assumptions are not realistic.

Exercise Flexibility

We live in a business era dominated by *hurdle rates* (the minimal rate of return an investment must achieve), discounted cash flow measurements, and other quantitative performance yardsticks. Anything that doesn't measure up gets the ax. The ruling logic is that projects that cannot forecast returns equal to or greater than the company's current return on capital will reduce that return—thus they should be abandoned. Many critics complain that this iron rule favors incremental projects that support existing businesses over true innovations, whose future rewards are difficult to know. Indeed, these rules sometimes produce perverse effects, as a manager in a textbook publishing company discovered several years ago. Looking back at the revenues generated by the first editions of his company's three top-selling books, which together accounted for over 30 percent of total revenues, this manager found that *not one* of those best sellers would have been published under his company's current quantitative rules.

"In each case," he said, "the first edition of our current best sellers enjoyed very modest sales. But someone decided to go ahead with new editions anyway, and each subsequent edition was more widely adopted. Today, those books are all in their tenth and twelfth editions, and are the biggest cash cows we have."

Be flexible as well when considering the size of new businesses developed through innovation. Even projects that legitimately forecast acceptable returns are terminated if anticipated revenues are judged "too small" relative to the business as a whole. For large companies, a new venture that cannot forecast annual revenues of $10 million within five years of commercialization is generally dropped. The logic: "It's too small for us to mess around with." Harvard Business School professor Rosabeth Moss Kanter cites the example of Time, Inc., the magazine division of Time Warner, as an example of this problem.[5] During the 1980s and early 1990s, Time was so intent on finding the next *Sports Illustrated* or *People*—two of its huge successes—that new magazine launches ground to a halt. No new concepts were found with sales magnitudes equal to those past ventures.

So what are leaders to do? Initial markets for truly innovative products and services are often small; though many have the potential to grow over time to the point where they eclipse the revenues of the established business. Assuming that supporting resources are available, leaders must periodically take calculated risks on projects that, though small, might surprise everyone by growing into future cash cows.

Don't Overlook Innovations in Processes, Finance, and Distribution

Companies are always looking for the new product and service breakthrough that will give their income statements a big boost. This appetite for new products (and services) is nourished by breathless stories in the business media: how the iPod sent Apple share prices through the roof, how 3M gets upward of 30 percent of annual revenues from products released in the past five years, how eBay made billions out of its online auction service, and so forth.

Innovative new products and services are surely important, but leaders should never overlook the importance of innovation in business processes, finance, distribution, the supply chain, and other functional areas. The reduced manufacturing costs that result from process improvements, for instance, can be as helpful to the bottom line as the launch of an innovative new product. Further, the risks associated with process innovation may be less. The product or service innovator faces two fundamental risks: First, "Can we make this work?" Second, "If it works, will the market accept it?" The process innovator must successfully address only the first of these questions.

Put People with the Right Stuff in Charge

Some of the most important decisions that senior executives make involve the selection of R&D managers. They are the people closest to the activities that determine the company's future products, processes, and services. But what types of people are most suitable? Generally, executives should look for people with four qualities:

- Strong technical backgrounds—they should have a good feel for the trajectories of technologies important to the company

- Familiarity with the strategic concerns of the organization

- Experience with customers and their problems

- Strong interpersonal and communication skills. As Rosabeth Moss Kanter has put it, "Innovations need connectors—people who know how to find partners in the mainstream business or in the outside world."[6] Many overlook that advice.

Create an Ambidextrous Organization

Michael Tushman and Charles O'Reilly propose that successful leaders of innovation create "ambidextrous" organizations—that is, organizations that can "get today's work done more effectively and

[also] anticipate tomorrow's discontinuities."[7] These are two very different and contradictory capabilities. Organizations that have both are capable of excelling in the present even as they create the future. Their leaders defend current product/technology positions through incremental innovation while simultaneously developing new ones that will either displace current offerings or address new markets.

Richard Leifer and his colleagues reached a similar conclusion in their study of radical innovation in established companies. In their view, the greatest challenge for senior management is balancing their focus on the short-term performance of the existing business as they pursue long-term growth through innovation.[8] These are two very different games, and few companies play both well. The source of the challenge is not hard to understand. Success in the current business is usually driven by certainty, efficiency, and cost control; the future business, on the other hand, is the product of an innovation process that is uncertain, inefficient, and costly. Not many executives can operate successfully in these two very different activities. Most are so absorbed with the current business that the future business is treated as a stepchild, attended to when time and resources permit.

The best way to create an ambidextrous organization is to:

1. **Assess where you are in terms of innovation trends:** Are your current products and technologies on the rapid upward slope of the S-curve, or are they in the mature phase of the curve? Do new technologies have the potential to undermine your business?

2. **Assess your company's operations:** Are they effective, fast, and efficient? Are major cost improvements possible through process innovation?

3. **Based on your answers to items 1 and 2, reorder your priorities and resources:** You need to be very good at both current operations and innovation.

Summing Up

While most idea generation and creativity takes place at midlevel and lower ranks, the organization's leaders play a key role. This chapter has explained what leaders can do to stimulate creativity and increase the pace of innovation. It is their responsibility to:

- Develop a culture that nurtures creativity and innovation

- Establish the strategic direction within which innovation should take place

- Improve the idea-to-commercialization process

Finally, the senior leadership must take responsibility for creating an ambidextrous organization—one that is effective at two very different activities: getting today's work done (operations) and anticipating the future. Few organizations do both well.

Writing a Business Plan

A *business plan* is a document that explains a business opportunity, identifies the market to be served, and provides details about how the organization plans to pursue it. Ideally, the business plan describes the unique qualifications that the team brings to the effort, explains the resources required for success, and provides a forecast of results over a reasonable time horizon.

If you are an entrepreneur, you'll need a business plan in order to obtain funding. Lenders and investors want to see a logical and coherent plan before putting their money at risk. Who wouldn't? If you are innovating within a corporation—or if you're an idea champion—you too will benefit from having a formal business plan. Like private lenders and venture capitalists, your management will want a full-blown story before they part with their money.

A good business plan:

- Makes the best case for the idea

- Avoids burying the exciting opportunity under a mountain of data

- Is engaging to read

- Gives prospective supporters the information they need to make a decision

This short appendix cannot impart all the information you need if you are to write a resource-winning plan, nor can it offer details of what every plan section should contain. You'll find those details in any of the many books currently available on this subject. It does, however, impart the serious purposes of a business plan and explain the key points that readers look for in the many plans that cross their desks. It is written from the perspective of an entrepreneurial company, but can also inform the business plan development of the corporate innovator.

Suggested Format

Figure A-1 contains a prototype format for a company we will call Lo-Carbo Foods Company, a manufacturer of packaged breakfast and snack foods having low carbohydrate levels. It aims to capitalize on the growing popularity in North America and Europe of low-carb diets. The company's research estimates that twenty-nine million Americans and eight million Europeans are now following low-carb diets, which U.S. government studies have confirmed to be effective in weight reduction and weight control.

There is nothing sacred about the format shown here. In fact, you would be wise to tailor your plan format to the likely interests of your readers, just as you would customize the résumé you develop

FIGURE A-1

Prototype business plan formal

Lo-Carbo incorporated business plan

when seeking employment. Thus, you should follow the first rule of every form of writing: Know your audience. The goal in every case is to give readers the information they need to make a decision.

Let's consider each major section of this document in greater detail.

Contents and Executive Summary

The Contents section (or table of contents) makes it easy for readers to see at a glance what the plan has to offer and where it can be located. The contents should be followed by an executive summary, a short section of two to three pages. In terms of selling your plan, this is the most important part of the entire document, so take the time to get it right. The executive summary is not a preface or an introduction; instead, it is a snapshot of the entire plan, something that explains your business to an intelligent reader in only a few minutes. A well-written executive summary captures the interest and attention of readers and prepares them for what follows.

The Opportunity

There is no point in pursuing an innovative business concept if the entrepreneur or idea champion has not identified a lucrative opportunity. Use this section to describe that opportunity: the market factors driving it, its current size, and its projected size in the years ahead. Describe the opportunity in terms that are clear and compelling.

Use this section also to highlight the economics underlying the opportunity and the factors that will drive its success, such as market penetration, product innovation, and so on. But don't get carried away. Keep it brief, focused, and upbeat. This is also a suitable place to cite the magnitude of the funding being sought and explain how it will be used in pursuing the opportunity.

Although it is important to document the opportunity with objective data, don't turn this section into a boring "data dump." Don't allow your compelling story to be buried under a mountain of facts.

Instead, summarize the data and explain its implications for investors. Put the actual documentation in an appendix.

The Product (or Service) Line and Its Strategy

Use this section to describe the company, explain how it is organized, and state its essential purpose. Don't forget to include a subsection about the goals of the company and its business strategy. Investors will want to know how you plan to grow. If there is a chance that the company will become a tempting acquisition target for a larger, less innovative competitor, mention this possibility. Here is an example:

Lo-Carbo has three goals:

1. To broaden its product line

2. To expand market penetration through stores and through a private labeling agreement with one of the major diet companies (currently in negotiations)

3. To expand the business to the point where it either becomes a dominant player in the low-carbohydrate food niche *or* is acquired by one of the packaged food industry giants.

If your products are not yet market-ready, you should reveal your plans for product rollouts. Also include an artist's rendering of the final physical product. If your products are market-ready, go beyond the written description; include high-quality photographs.

Also include in this or a separate section a discussion of the company's strategy. Strategy is about differentiation and competitive advantage. Explain what is different about your approach to the marketplace and how that difference will give it a sustainable competitive advantage.

The Management Team

Investors are keen to know about the people behind the business, whom they see as key assets. Specifically, what experiences or qualifications do they bring to the enterprise?

- Where are the founders from?

- Where were they educated?

- Where have they worked—and for whom?

- What have they accomplished—professionally and personally—in the past?

- What experience do they have that is directly relevant to the opportunity they are pursuing?

Put the details of their backgrounds into an appendix to prevent readers from getting bogged down.

Organization

Most plans use an organization chart to indicate the reporting relationships among key personnel. A table indicating names, titles, and salaries is also useful.

Assuming that your company is a corporation, this is also an appropriate place to identify the board of directors. You should indicate the names of board members, their positions on the board, their

About Intellectual Property

Is your competitive advantage based on a proprietary technology or process? Is that technology or process patented or "patentable"? Does the company own patents, copyrights, or valuable trademarks? If it does, when will they expire?

Many businesses are formed around one or another piece of intellectual property. Some are key assets that impact competitive advantage over a period of time. Readers of your plan will want to know what steps you've taken to protect that property and to keep technical and market know-how within the organization, where it will produce revenues and profits for investors.

professional backgrounds, and their history of involvement with the company.

Recruiting board members should be a matter of the highest importance. You want people who have abundant business experience and, if technology is essential to the business, considerable scientific or engineering know-how. Board members should also be respected in the broader business community. Their capabilities and integrity will speak volumes to whoever reads your business plan, financiers in particular.

Marketing Plan

If the "people" section of your business plan gets the most attention from readers, the marketing plan runs a close second. Investors know that marketing is the activity most associated with success or failure. An attractive product or service is essential, but a company will fail if it cannot connect with customers. A sound and realistic marketing plan is the best assurance that a solid customer connection will be made. The plan should be clear about all aspects of marketing, including the following:

- Identification of customers

- The number of potential customers and potential sales revenues

- The requirements of various customer segments

- The importance of purchase convenience, rapid delivery, product customization, and so on for these segments

- Ways to effectively access each segment—through distributors, a captive sales force, direct mail, e-commerce, or whatever

- Appropriate sales and promotion approaches

- An analysis of how purchase decisions are made

- Customer price sensitivity

- The cost of acquiring and retaining customers

- The strengths and weaknesses of competitors and ways that competitors are likely to react when the company enters the market

For your plan to be credible, these issues should be supported with solid market intelligence. Summarize that supporting intelligence here, and refer readers to whatever market research you've provided in the appendix.

Operating Plan

Whether you're in the business of designing products, manufacturing them, acting as a distributor, or running an e-commerce site, you are faced with a host of operational issues. What supplier relationships do you have or envision? How much inventory will be required? If you are a manufacturer, will you follow a job shop or continuous flow operation? Which day-to-day operating chores will be handled internally, and which will be outsourced?

An operations plan considers the many details of converting inputs to outputs that customers value. What is your plan?

Financial Plan

If a company is already operating, it will have (or should have) a set of financial statements: a *balance sheet*, an *income statement*, and a *cash flow statement*. In a nutshell, the balance sheet describes what the company owns—its assets—and how those assets have been financed (through liabilities and the funds of the current owners) as of a particular date.

The income statement reveals the company's revenues, what it spent to gain those revenues, and the interest and taxes it paid over a specified period. Finally, the cash flow statement tells readers the sources and uses of cash during the same period. Together, these three financial statements reveal much to the trained eye of potential investors.

Generally, it's best to place the full financial statements in the appendix to your business plan. Use this space for key data from those statements—data that will give readers the big picture of your business and its intended future. Key among these data are your sales and expense projections, described earlier in this book as a pro forma income statement.

Style

Every business plan is a combination of style and substance. Not being wordsmiths, most entrepreneurs concentrate on the substance and shortchange the style. That's unfortunate, because inattention to style makes a plan dull and difficult to read.

One remedy is to work with a writer who has experience in business plan writing. Another is to be your own wordsmith and observe the rules of good writing: Use words sparingly, keep sentences simple, make the most of design elements, and use graphics judiciously.

Use Words Sparingly

In the business world, shorter is always better if it communicates the required information. So heed Rule 17 in Strunk and White's timeless *Elements of Style*, and omit needless words. "Vigorous writing is concise. A sentence should contain no unnecessary words; a paragraph no unnecessary sentences; for the same reason that a drawing should have no unnecessary lines and a machine no unnecessary parts. This requires not that the writer make all his sentences short, or that he avoid all detail and treat his subjects only in outline, but that every word tells."[1]

This quotation is itself a perfect model of their rule: every word makes a contribution. Economy of words has two big benefits for the business plan writer: your key messages will stand out, and economy of words saves your readers valuable time.

Use Simple Sentences

The sentence is the basic unit of written expression. Most sentences make a statement. The statement can be simple or complex. Consider these:

1. The growing popularity of low-carbohydrate diets has created a business opportunity for makers of low-carb foods.

2. On the one hand we witness rising levels of obesity among children and adults, both in North America and in Western Europe, which in turn have increased the popularity of low-carb diets, which in turn have created a business opportunity for Lo-Carb Company and other makers of low-carb foods.

The first sentence, unlike the second, is spare and to the point. It will more likely register with readers. It does not contain all the information found in the second. If that information is important, it should be provided in a separate sentence.

Packing more information into each sentence is not necessarily bad, nor does it violate the rules of grammar if done properly. However, complex sentences make the reader work harder and may create confusion. As a writer, your challenge is to know when a sentence has reached its optimal carrying capacity.

Use Design Elements to Lighten the Reader's Load

Readers of your business plan are busy people who have learned to skim; they drill down only to what they believe to be relevant details. You can facilitate their skimming through the use of design elements: include headings, subheads, and short blocks of text. Even white space can be used as a design element. All are useful in long documents.

A Caution on Design Elements

Don't get carried away. Word processing software gives you an arsenal of design features: boldface, italics, dozens of font sizes and styles, clip art, chart-making tools, and so forth. Used judiciously, these add to the appearance and readability of your text. Overuse them, however, and you will create the opposite effect and make your work appear amateurish. So keep it simple.

Final Thoughts

As you develop your business plan, always keep the interests of your readers in mind. Put yourself in their place. Your audience is looking for convincing evidence that you have found a real business opportunity—one with substantial growth possibilities. Considering the risks they will be taking with their money, they want to see major upside potential.

Your plan's readers will also be looking for clear indications that you have done your homework—that you understand the market, have targeted the right customers, and have developed a sound strategy for profitably transacting business with them. Prospective investors want assurance that you and the management team have the knowledge, experience, and drive to turn an opportunity into a profitable business. And what is important to potential lenders and investors should be just as important to you. So as you write your plan, stop periodically and ask yourself, Is this a real opportunity? Do I understand the market and the customers I hope to attract? Can we really make this thing work?

Finally, tell your readers how they will get their money out of the company.

Investors want an exit strategy: a buyout by management, an acquisition by another company, an initial public offering of shares, and so on. Even if you plan to be in the business for the long haul, your investors want liquidity at some point—and the sooner the better.

Workplace Assessment Checklist

How friendly is your workplace to creativity and innovation? This checklist will help you make an assessment. Suggestion: photocopy the checklist and have several people fill in the ratings independently, then compare answers. This will help you see the workplace—and yourself—as others see it.

Note: The official Harvard Business Essentials Web site, www.elearning.hbsp.org/businesstools, offers free interactive versions of this checklist and other tools introduced in this series.

Dimension	Rating		
	Adequate	A strength	Needs improvement
Your leadership style			
I can describe my own preferred style of thinking and working.			
I have talked with members of my group about their preferred modes of problem solving.			
I encourage intellectual conflict within my group.			
When group members disagree, I help them determine the source of their differences.			
When communicating with others, I take into consideration their preferred thinking style.			
Diversity of styles			
I am aware of the creative value of diverse thinking styles, and try to incorporate this diversity in teams.			
I actively seek out or hire people with diverse backgrounds and thinking styles.			
Our group recognizes the conflict that creative abrasion can cause, but also recognizes its value.			
We have taken formal diagnostic tests to identify thinking or learning styles, and discussed the results of these assessments.			
Your work group			
The majority never ignores the minority opinions in my work group.			
I have added someone to my work group specifically because he/she brings a fresh perspective.			
Our work environment supports those who think differently from the majority.			
The thinking styles, skills, and experiences of my work group's members are diverse and balanced.			
I actively look for group members whose thinking styles differ from my own.			
I help my group establish and agree upon a clear project goal at the start of each project.			
My group has formally agreed-upon behavior guidelines for how they should work together and treat each other			
The psychological environment			
I support people taking intelligent risks, and do not penalize them when they fail.			
There are opportunities for people to take on assignments that involve risk and stretch their potential.			
We openly discuss risk taking, assess the risk potential of projects, and make contingency plans or identify risk management strategies.			

Dimension	Adequate	Rating A strength	Needs improvement
The psychological environment			
Rewards and/or recognition are given for creative ideas.			
As long as they show learning from the experience, group members are not penalized for experimentation and risk taking.			
The physical workspace			
Our workspace includes stimulating objects such as journals, art, and other items that are not directly related to our business.			
I have made changes to our physical workspace to improve communication and creative interaction.			
I provide group members with a wide variety of traditional and nontraditional communication tools (e-mail, whiteboards, crayons and paper, etc.).			
Group members are encouraged to make their workspaces reflect their individuality.			
Our workspace includes *both* areas for boisterous interaction and areas for quiet reflection.			
Bringing in outsiders or alternative perspectives			
Our group makes visits to people outside the division or organization in order to find different perspectives and ideas.			
Our group has observed customers actually using our product or service *in their own environment*.			
Our group has observed our customers' customers using our product or service *in their own environment*.			
I have arranged for speakers from other industries to come talk to or work with my group.			
Our group has observed people using competitors' products or services.			
Our group has benchmarked the functions and characteristics of our products, services, or internal processes against an industry other than our own.			
Promoting group convergence			
I encourage group members to bring up and discuss non-work-related subjects when they interfere with work.			
When a project has been completed, I hold a debrief meeting to determine specifically what to do differently (or the same) the next time.			
When I hold a debrief meeting, I always make sure that all members can be present.			
When my group is stuck on a problem, I make sure they get "down time" or time off to step back, relax, and allow their subconscious minds to work.			

	Rating		
Dimension	**Adequate**	**A strength**	**Needs improvement**
Promoting group convergence			
At the end of a project, I provide a way for my group to celebrate and rejuvenate.			
Project schedules allow enough time for group brainstorming and discussion of ideas.			

Adapted from multimedia CD *Managing Groups for Creativity and Innovation* (Boston: Harvard Business School Publishing, 2000). © 2000 by the President and Fellows of Harvard College and its licensors. All rights reserved.

Notes

Introduction

1. Lynn White, Jr., *Medieval Technology and Social Change* (Oxford, England: Oxford University Press, 1962), 14–38.

Chapter 1

1. The story of the SiGe chip and its innovator is ably told in various sections of Richard Leifer et al., *Radical Innovation: How Mature Companies Can Outsmart Upstarts* (Boston: Harvard Business School Press, 2000).

2. Ibid., 5.

3. Lee A. Sage, *Winning the Innovation Race* (New York: Wiley, 2000), 7.

4. Michael L. Tushman and Charles A. O'Reilly III, *Winning Through Innovation* (Boston: Harvard Business School Press, 1997), 160–161.

5. See George S. Day, "Closing the Growth Gap: Balancing BIG I and small i Innovation," *Knowledge@Wharton*, February 1, 2007, http://knowledge.wharton.upenn.edu/paper.cfm?paperID=1344.

6. Leifer et al., *Radical Innovation*.

7. Ibid.

8. James M. Utterback, *Mastering the Dynamics of Innovation: How Companies Can Seize Opportunities in the Face of Technological Change* (Boston: Harvard Business School Press, 1994), 106–116.

9. Procter & Gamble's development of the disposable diaper is told in Oscar Schisgall, *Eyes on Tomorrow: The Evolution of Procter & Gamble* (Chicago: J.G. Ferguson Publishing Co., 1981) 216–220.

Chapter 2

1. Peter F. Drucker, "The Discipline of Innovation," *Harvard Business Review*, May–June 1985, 65–67.

2. Greg. A. Stevens and James Hurley, "3,000 Raw Ideas = 1 Commercial Success!" *Research—Technology Management*, May–June 1997.

3. George Beall, from a speech delivered at the Industrial Research Institute Fall Meeting in San Jose, California, October 2001.

4. "Solving the Innovator's Dilemma," *Product Development Best Practices Report*, May 2000, http://www.managementroundtable.com/PDBPR/strategyn.html.

5. G. L. Lilien, P. D. Morrison, K. Searls, M. Sonnack, and E. von Hippel, "Performance Assessment of the Lead User Idea-Generation Process for New Product Development." *Management Science* 48, no. 8, (2002): 1042–1059.

6. The Posse Ride experience is recorded in multimedia case format in Susan Fournier, Sylvia Sensiper, James McAlexander, and John Schouten, "Building Brand Community on the Harley-Davidson Posse Ride," Harvard Business School Case no. 501009 (Boston: Harvard Business School Publishing, 2000).

7. Podcast of interview with David Kelley, http://iinnovate.blogspot.com/2006/08/david-kelley-founder-of-ideo.html.

8. For a full discussion of the Honda Element cases, see chapters six and eight in Marc H. Meyer, *The Fast Path to Corporate Growth* (New York: Oxford University Press, 2007).

9. Dorothy Leonard and Jeffrey F. Rayport, "Spark Innovation Through Empathetic Design," *Harvard Business Review*, November–December 1997, 102–113.

10. Richard Leifer et al., *Radical Innovation: How Mature Companies Can Outsmart Upstarts* (Boston: Harvard Business School Press, 2000), 142–155.

11. Lee A. Sage, *Winning the Innovation Race* (New York: Wiley, 2000), 15–16.

12. Darrell Rigby and Chris Zook, "Open Market Innovation," *Harvard Business Review*, October 2002, 80–89.

13. Ibid.

14. Larry Huston and Nabil Sakkab, "Connect and Develop: Inside Procter & Gamble's New Model for Innovation," *Harvard Business Review*, March 2006.

15. Albert Shapero, "The Management of Creative Professionals," *Research-Technology Management* 28, no. 2 (March–April 1985): 23–28.

16. Edward Roberts and Alan Fusfeld, "Critical Functions: Needed Roles in the Innovation Process," in *The Human Side of Managing Technological Innovation*, ed. Ralph Katz (New York: Oxford University Press, 1997), 279.

17. Robert I. Sutton, *Weird Ideas That Work* (New York: Free Press, 2002), 94–103.

18. This method is described in detail in Genrich Altshuller, *And Suddenly the Inventor Appeared: TRIZ, the Theory of Inventive Problem Solving*, 2nd

ed., trans. Lev Shulyak (Worcester, MA: Technical Innovation Center, Inc., 1996).

19. For a more complete description of catchball, see George Labovitz and Victor Rosansky, *The Power of Alignment: How Great Companies Stay Centered and Accomplish Extraordinary Things* (New York: Wiley, 1997), 90–92.

Chapter 3

1. Mark Rice and Gina Colarelli O'Connor, "Opportunity Recognition and Breakthrough Innovation in Large Established Firms," *California Management Review* 43, no. 2 (Winter 2001): 96.

2. For more on DuPont's experience with Biomax, see Richard Leifer et al., *Radical Innovation: How Mature Companies Can Outsmart Upstarts* (Boston: Harvard Business School Press, 2001), 12–16.

3. Rice and O'Connor, "Opportunity Recognition and Breakthrough Innovation in Large Established Firms," 105.

4. This discussion is based on W. Chan Kim and Renée Mauborgne, "Knowing a Winning Idea When You See One," *Harvard Business Review*, September–October 2000, 129–136, 138.

Chapter 4

1. See Richard Leifer et al., *Radical Innovation: How Mature Companies Can Outsmart Upstarts* (Boston: Harvard Business School Press, 2000), 38–39.

2. Michael D. Watkins, "The Power to Persuade," Note 9-800-323 (Boston: Harvard Business School Publishing, revised July 24, 2008).

Chapter 5

1. Greg A. Stevens and James Burley, "3000 Raw Ideas = 1 Commercial Success!" *Research-Technology Management* 40, no. 3 (May–June 1997): 16–27.

2. Nicholas Bloch, Dara Gruver, and David Cooper, "Slimming Innovation Pipelines to Fatten Their Returns," *Harvard Management Update*, August 2007.

3. For a more complete development of this issue, see Don Reinertsen, "There Is No Fun in the Funnel," *Product Development Best Practices Report*, October 1999, http://www.managementroundtable.com/PDBPR/Funnell.html.

4. Robert G. Cooper, "Stage-Gate Systems: A New Tool for Managing New Products," *Business Horizons*, May–June 1990, 45–54.

5. Robert G. Cooper, "Selecting Winning New Product Projects," *Journal of Product Innovation Management* 2, no. 1 (March 1985): 35.

6. Clayton M. Christensen, interview with HBS Publishing, October 8, 1998, www.hbsp.harvard.edu/products/pressbooks/innovator/qa/html.

7. Clayton M. Christensen, Stephen P. Kaufamn, and Willy C. Shih, "Innovation Killers: How Financial Tools Destroy Your Capacity to Do New Things," *Harvard Business Review*, January 2008.

8. Rita Gunther McGrath and Ian C. MacMillan, 'Discovery Driven Planning," *Harvard Business Review*, July–August 1995.

9. George S. Day, "Is It Real? Can We Win? Is It Worth Doing? Managing Risk and Reward in an Innovation Portfolio," *Harvard Business Review*, December 2007.

Chapter 6

1. Adam M. Brandenburger and Harborne W. Stuart Jr., "Value-based Strategy," *Journal of Economics & Management Strategy* (January 2005): 5–14.

2. David Bovet and Joseph Martha, *Value Nets: Breaking the Supply Chain to Unlock Hidden Profits* (New York: Wiley, 2000), 30.

3. For more on USAA, see Tom Teal, "Service Comes First: An Interview with USAA's Robert F. McDermott," *Harvard Business Review*, September–October 1991, 116–127.

4. "USAA Tops in Customer Survey Again," *San Antonio News*, June 27, 2007.

5. Michael E. Porter, "What Is Strategy?" *Harvard Business Review*, November–December 1996, 61–78.

Chapter 7

1. Carl von Clausewitz, *On War*, ed. Anatol Rapoport (London: Penguin Books, 1968).

2. Marc H. Meyer and Alvin P. Lehnerd, *The Power of Product Platforms* (New York: The Free Press, 1997), xii.

3. Ibid., 5–15.

Chapter 8

1. See Richard Foster, *Innovation: The Attacker's Advantage* (New York: Summit Books, 1986).

2. Michael L. Tushman and Charles A. O'Reilly III, *Winning Through Innovation* (Boston: Harvard Business School Press, 1997), 17.

3. Jay Paap and Ralph Katz, "Anticipating Disruptive Innovation," *Research-Technology Management* 47, no. 5 (September–October 2004): 13–22.

Chapter 9

1. Joseph L. Bower and Clayton M. Christensen, "Disruptive Technology: Catching the Next Wave," *Harvard Business Review*, January–February 1995.

2. Currently, the best advice for leveraging existing technology to new customer and new uses can be found in Marc H. Meyer, *The Fast Path to Corporate Growth* (New York: Oxford University Press, 2007).

3. Clayton M. Christensen, Scott D. Anthony and Erik A. Roth, *Seeing What's Next: Using Theories of Innovation to Predict Industry Change* (Boston: Harvard Business School Press, 2004), 4.

4. James R. Bright, "Evaluating Signals of Technological Change," *Harvard Business Review*, January–February 1970, 6 ; also see James R. Bright and James W. Brown, "Monitoring for Technological Change," *Business Horizons*, October 1972, 5–15.

5. Clayton M. Christensen, interview with HBS Publishing, October 8, 1998, www.hbsp.harvard.edu/products/pressbooks/innovator/qa/html.

Chapter 10

1. Robert G. Cooper, "Your NPD Portfolio May Be Harmful to Your Business Health," *PDMA Visions*, April 2005.

2. George S. Day, "Is It Real? Can We Win? Is It Worth Doing: Managing Risk and Reward in an Innovation Portfolio," *Harvard Business Review*, December 2007. As described by Day, the risk matrix "was developed from many sources, including long-buried consulting reports by A. T. Kearney and other firms," and other literature.

3. For a more complete discussion of top-down versus bottom-up strategy, see Eric Mankin, "Top Down Innovation at GE," at http://www.babsoninsight.com/contentmgr/showdetails.php/id/847.

Chapter 11

1. Graham Wallas, *The Art of Thought* (London: J. Cape, 1926). Modern readers can find a discussion of Wallas's four-stage process in Albert Shapero, "Managing Creative Professionals," *Research-Technology Management* 28, no. 2 (March–April 1985): 23–28.

2. Robert H. Dennard, "Creativity in the 2000s and Beyond," *Research-Technology Management* 43, no. 6 (November–December 2000): 23–25.

3. Shapero, "Managing Creative Professionals."

4. Ibid.

5. Teresa M. Amabile, "How to Kill Creativity," *Harvard Business Review*, September–October 1998, 77–87.

6. Dava Sobel, *Longitude: The True Story of a Lone Genius Who Solved the Greatest Scientific Problem of His Time* (New York: Walker & Company, 1995).

7. Amabile, "How to Kill Creativity."

8. Leonard. S. Cutler, "Creativity: Essential to Technological Innovation," *Research-Technology Management* 43, no. 6 (November–December 2000): 29–30.

Chapter 12

1. Teresa Amabile, Constance Hadley, and Steven Kramer, "Creativity Under the Gun," *Harvard Business Review*, August 2002, 57.

2. Ralph Katz, "Managing Creative Performance in R&D Teams," in *The Human Side of Managing Technological Innovation*, 2nd ed., ed. Ralph Katz (New York: Oxford University Press, 2007), 161.

3. Ibid., 163.

Chapter 13

1. Ben W. Heineman, Jr. "Inspiring Innovation," *Harvard Business Review*, August 2002, 49.

2. Ibid., 40.

3. For R&D labs definitive work in this area is Thomas J. Allen, "Communication Networks in R&D Laboratories," reprinted in *The Human Side of Managing Technological Innovation*, 2nd ed., ed. Ralph Katz (New York: Oxford University Press, 2004), 298–308.

4. Lee A. Sage, *Winning the Innovation Race* (New York: Wiley, 2000), 150–151.

5. For an excellent description of the Xerox–L.L. Bean cases, see Gregory H. Watson, *Strategic Benchmarking: How to Rate Your Company's Performance Against the World's Best* (New York: John Wiley & Sons, Inc., 1993), 149–167.

6. Richard Leifer, et al., *Radical Innovation: How Mature Companies Can Outsmart Upstarts* (Boston: Harvard Business School Press, 2000), 162–163.

7. See Turid Horgen, Donald A. Schön, William L. Porter, and Michael L. Joroff, *Excellence by Design* (New York: John Wiley & Sons, Inc., 1998).

8. Thomas J. Allen, "Communication Networks in R&D Labs," *R&D Management* 1 (1971): 14–21.

9. http://solutions.3m.com/wps/portal/3M/en_US/our/company/information/history/McKnight-principles/.

Chapter 14

1. Michael L. Tushman and Charles A. O'Reilly III, *Winning Through Innovation* (Boston: Harvard Business School Press, 1997, 33–34.

2. Michael Beer, "Leading Change," class note 9-488-037 (Boston: Harvard Business School Publishing, revised 15 May 1991), 2.

3. Lewis S. Edelheit, "Perspective on GE Research & Development," *Research-Technology Management* 47, no. 1 (January–February, 2004): 49–55.

4. Steven C. Wheelwright and Kim B. Clark, *Revolutionizing Product Development* (New York: Free Press, 1992), 22–34.

5. Rosabeth Moss Kanter, "Innovation: The Classic Traps," *Harvard Business Review*, November 2006.

6. Ibid.

7. Tushman and O'Reilly, *Winning Through Innovation*, 219.

8. Richard Leifer et al., *Radical Innovation: How Mature Companies Can Outsmart Upstarts* (Boston: Harvard Business School Press, 2000).

Appendix A

1. William J. Strunk, with E. B. White, *The Elements of Style*, 4th ed. (Boston: Allyn & Bacon, 1998), rule 17.

Glossary

BREAKEVEN ANALYSIS: A financial method for determining how much (or how much more) you need to sell of a product or service in order to pay for a fixed investment—in other words, at what point you will break even on the cash flow produced by the new product or service.

BREAKTHROUGH INNOVATION: See *Radical innovation.*

BUSINESS CASE: The information and argumentation needed to demonstrate the merits of an innovative idea to management and other stakeholders.

CATCHBALL: A cross-functional method for accomplishing two things: idea enrichment/improvement and buy-in among participants.

CHAMPION: A person who assumes responsibility for moving a promising innovative idea or project along a path toward the market. The champion need not be the idea's creator, but must have the enthusiasm and commitment needed to promote and implement it on the road to success.

COMMUNITY OF INTEREST: An informal group whose members share an interest in some technology or application.

CONTRIBUTION MARGIN: The amount of money that every sold unit contributes to paying for fixed costs. It is defined as net unit revenue minus variable (or direct) costs per unit.

CONVERGENT THINKING: Thinking that evaluates new ideas to determine which are genuinely novel and worth pursuing.

COST OF CAPITAL: The weighted average cost of the organization's different sources of capital, both debt and equity, expressed as a percentage.

CREATIVITY: A process of developing and expressing novel ideas that are likely to be useful.

DIFFERENTIATION: Deliberately setting one's product or service apart from those of rivals in a way that customers value.

DISCONTINUOUS INNOVATION: See *Radical innovation.*

DISCOUNTED CASH FLOW (DCF) ANALYSIS: A method for determining the monetary value of a commercial idea or cash flows over a particular span of time based on time-value-of-money concepts.

DISCOUNT RATE: In discounted cash flow analysis, the annual rate, expressed as a percentage, at which a future payment or series of payments is reduced to its present value.

DISCOVERY-DRIVEN PLANNING: A method of evaluation in which decision makers focus their attention on the assumptions that must prove true if the venture or innovation is to reach an acceptable level of profitability.

DISRUPTIVE INNOVATION: An innovation that brings to the market a new and different value proposition with the potential to upset the status quo in a competitive market. A term coined by Clayton Christenson.

DIVERGENT THINKING: Thinking that breaks away from familiar or established ways of seeing and doing.

EMPATHETIC DESIGN: An idea-generating technique whereby innovators observe how people use existing products and services in their own environments.

EXPERIENCE CURVE: A concept that holds that the cost of doing a repetitive task decreases by some percentage each time the cumulative volume of production doubles.

EXTRINSIC REWARD: A reward that appeals to a person's desire for attainment distinct from the work itself: a cash bonus, a promotion, or stock options.

FIXED COSTS: Costs that stay mostly the same, no matter how many units of a product or service are sold—costs such as the cost of product development, insurance, management salaries, and rent or lease payments.

GROUPTHINK: A phenomenon often observed in cohesive or homogeneous groups that produces unanimity of opinion, resistance to contrary viewpoints, and antagonism to group members who disagree with the prevailing view.

HURDLE RATE: The minimal rate of return that all investments for a particular enterprise must achieve.

IDEA FUNNEL: A concept used in product development to illustrate how many innovative ideas are gradually reduced down to a very few that proceed to commercialization.

INCREMENTAL INNOVATION: Innovation that either improves on something that already exists or reconfigures an existing form or technology to service some other purpose. In this sense, it is innovation that exploits some existing form.

INFLUENCER: An individual who provides advice and information to key stakeholders and decision makers.

INNOVATION: The embodiment, combination, and/or synthesis of knowledge in original, relevant, valued new products, processes, or services.

INTERNAL RATE OF RETURN (IRR):   The discount rate at which the NPV of an investment equals zero.

INTRINSIC REWARD: A reward that appeals to a person's desire for self-actualization, curiosity, enjoyment, or interest in the work itself.

KAIZEN: A philosophy of continuous process improvement that encourages everyone, at every level, to seek out ways to improve what they are doing.

LEAD USER: A company or individual whose needs are far ahead of market trends. Lead users often modify off-the-shelf products to suit their special needs.

NET PRESENT VALUE (NPV):   The present value of one or more future cash flows less any initial investment.

NETWORK EFFECT: A phenomenon in which the value of a product increases as more products are sold and the network of users increases. The telephone was an innovation that benefited from the network effect.

OPEN MARKET INNOVATION: The practice of reaching outside one's company for new product and service ideas.

OPINION LEADER: A person respected for his or her expertise, judgment, and insights. This is the "go-to" person to whom others turn when seeking information or making decisions. The opinion leader's endorsement of an idea lends credibility and helps accelerate its acceptance.

OPPORTUNITY RECOGNITION: A mental process that answers the question "Does this idea represent real value to current or potential customers?"

PERCEPTUAL MAPPING: A market research tool used to compare products or product ideas against the perceptions of customers. A perceptual map is (usually) a two-dimensional space on which alternative product or product ideas are plotted against their attributes or the primary needs of customers.

PORTFOLIO MANAGEMENT: A methodology widely used by both corporations and individual business divisions to create a proper mix of new product/service or technology projects.

PREFERRED THINKING STYLE: The unconscious way a person looks at and interacts with the world. When faced with a problem or dilemma, a person will usually approach it through a preferred thought style.

PROCESS REENGINEERING: An improvement concept that aims for large breakthrough change—either through wholesale change or the elimination of existing processes.

PRODUCT (SERVICE) PLATFORM: The functional core of a product—usually described as the subsystems and interfaces that form a common structure from which many derivative products can be efficiently developed and produced.

RADICAL INNOVATION: An innovation that represents something new to the world and a departure from existing technology or method. Also referred to as *breakthrough* and *discontinuous* innovation.

S-CURVE: A curve plotted on a two-dimensional plane that models the performance or cost characteristics of a technology change with time and continued investments. The plan's horizontal axis reflects time and investment, while the vertical axis indicates product/service performance or cost competitiveness.

SKUNK WORKS: A team of people brought together to generate an innovative solution or to solve a particular problem. In some cases, these are sited in remote settings to keep team members focused on their mission, to minimize interference from the rest of the organizations, or to maintain secrecy.

SPONSOR: Usually a senior person who holds a position of power and who controls some level of resources. This person often provides help with implementation problems and suggests ways in which the champion can present an idea most effectively to management. The sponsor frequently works behind the scenes to supply resources and to protect it from premature extermination.

STAGE-GATE SYSTEM: The stage-gate system is an alternating series of development stages and assessment gates that aims for early elimination of losing ideas and faster time-to-market for potential winners.

SUSTAINING INNOVATION: An innovation that improves the performance of established products. The term was coined by Clayton Christenson.

TEAM ROOM: A dedicated physical space within which full- or part-time members of a work team can congregate to do their work, share information, brainstorm, and so forth. It serves as a central "node" in the communication network that holds participants together and facilitates the information and idea sharing.

TRIZ: Acronym for *t*heory of *i*nventive *p*roblem *s*olving, which systematically solves problems and creates innovation by identifying and eliminating technical contradictions.

VARIABLE COSTS: Those costs that change with the number of units produced and sold; examples include utilities, labor, and the costs of raw materials.

For Further Reading

Altshuller, Genrich; Lev Shulyak, translator. *And Suddenly the Inventor Appeared: TRIZ, the Theory of Inventive Problem Solving*, 2nd edition. Worcester, MA: Technical Innovation Center, Inc., 1996. Altshuller's take on how to become an inventor and how to solve technical problems.

Csikszentmihályi, Mihály. *Creativity: Flow and the Psychology of Discovery and Invention*. New York: Harper Collins, 1996. Csikszentmihályi focuses on the creativity of exceptional people—the paradoxical traits they possess and the unique aspects of their development over the life cycle—but he also suggests ways for enhancing creativity in everyday life.

Davis, Howard, and Richard Scase. *Managing Creativity: The Dynamics of Work and Organization*. Buckingham, UK: Open University Press, 2001. The creative industries are a growing economic as well as cultural force. This book investigates their organizational dynamics and shows how companies structure their work processes to incorporate creative employees' needs for autonomy while at the same time controlling and coordinating their output.

Florida, Richard, and Jim Goodnight. "Managing for Creativity." *Harvard Business Review* OnPoint Enhanced Edition. Boston: Harvard Business School Publishing, 2007. How do you accommodate the complex and chaotic nature of the creative process while increasing efficiency, improving quality, and raising productivity? Most businesses haven't figured this out. A notable exception is SAS Institute, the world's largest privately held software company. SAS has learned how to harness the creative energies of all its stakeholders, including its customers, software developers, managers, and support staff. Its framework for managing creativity rests on three guiding principles. First, help employees do their best work by keeping them intellectually engaged and by removing distractions. Second, make managers responsible for sparking creativity and eliminate arbitrary distinctions between "suits" and "creatives." And third, engage customers as creative partners so you can deliver superior products.

Harvard Business School Publishing. *Continuous Innovation: No Genius Required. Harvard Business Review* OnPoint Collection. Boston: Harvard Business School Publishing, 2001. This *Harvard Business Review* On-Point Collection shows you how to approach innovation by systematically: (1) generating new possibilities through applying old, proven ideas to new situations; (2) gathering additional ideas by identifying and learning from individuals and companies well ahead of market trends; and (3) testing the merits of those ideas through rapid, inexpensive experimentation.

Harvard Business School Publishing. "Debriefing Luc de Brabandere: Boost Your Company's Creativity." *Harvard Management Update*, April 2006. Today, popular tastes mutate constantly and technologies advance at a blistering pace. Businesses must continually innovate to keep up. But leaders who can't detect and respond to rumblings of change—that is, who can't be creative—stand little chance of generating these innovations. The key to creativity, according to Luc de Brabandere, a partner in The Boston Consulting Group, is learning to articulate and change the stereotypes that limit us. In this debriefing, he outlines four rules managers can follow to circumvent these blocks and hone creative powers.

Harvard Business School Publishing. *Harvard Business Review on Breakthrough Thinking.* Boston: Harvard Business School Press, 1999. This collection of *Harvard Business Review* articles highlights leading ideas for incorporating the power of creativity into your strategic outlook.

Kanter, Rosabeth Moss. "The Middle Manager as Innovator." *Harvard Business Review* OnPoint Enhanced Edition. Boston: Harvard Business School Publishing, 2001. Kanter's study of 165 effective middle managers in five leading corporations explores creative managerial contributions and the conditions that stimulate innovation. This article points out that enterprising, entrepreneurial middle managers share a number of characteristics: comfort with change, clarity of direction, thoroughness, a participative management style, as well as persuasiveness, persistence, and discretion.

Katz, Ralph, editor. *The Human Side of Managing Technological Innovation*, 2nd edition. New York: Oxford University Press, 2002. This collection of articles hits all the bases that a manager of innovation must understand, such as how to motivate R&D professionals and how to manage innovative groups, project teams, and organizational projects. It's a handy reference for the important people part of innovation.

Kim, W. Chan and Renée Mauborgne, "Knowing a Winning Idea When You See One," *Harvard Business Review*, September-October 2000. Identifying which business ideas have real commercial potential is fraught with uncertainty. This article introduces three tools that managers can use to help strip away some of that uncertainty. The first is the buyer utility map (described in chapter 3 of this book). The second, the price corridor of the mass, identifies what price will unlock the greatest number of customers. The third, the business model guide, offers a framework for figuring out whether and how a company can profitably deliver the new idea at the targeted price.

Laduke, Patty, Tom Andrews, and Keith Yamashita. "Igniting a Passion for Innovation." *Strategy & Innovation*, July–August 2003. Innovation isn't simply about a great new thing; it often requires change, and change encounters barriers—some quite powerful. These authors describe how innovators can overcome those barriers by explaining both the why and what: a compelling purpose for an innovation (the *why*) that speaks to both the hearts and minds of one's audience is often the key to success.

Leifer, Richard, Christopher M. McDermott, Gina Colarelli O'Connor, Lois S. Peters, Mark Rice, and Robert W. Veryzer. *Radical Innovation: How Mature Companies Can Outsmart Upstarts*. Boston: Harvard Business School Press, 2000. This book reveals the patterns through which game-changing innovation occurs in large, established companies, and identifies the new managerial competencies firms need to make radical innovation happen. The authors, experts in a variety of areas such as entrepreneurship, R&D management, product design, marketing, organizational behavior, and operations and project management, distill a comprehensive, interdisciplinary approach to mastering each of these challenges, from the conceptualization of viable ideas to the commercialization of radical innovations.

Leonard, Dorothy, and Walter Swap. *When Sparks Fly: Igniting Creativity in Groups*. Boston: Harvard Business School Press, 1999. Where do the best creative ideas come from? Most managers assume that it's the readily identifiable "creative types" that offer the quickest route to out-of-the-box, breakthrough thinking, and if you don't have an eccentric genius on your team, your group is doomed to mediocrity. Yet, say Leonard and Swap, most innovations today spring from well-led group interactions. In this book, the authors reveal that any group—if designed and managed effectively—can produce more innovative services, products, and processes. Unlike most books on creativity, *When Sparks Fly* focuses on the process as it applies to groups of people who may not fit the stereotype of right-brained "creatives." Leonard and Swap offer managers strategies for generating the group dynamics that lie at the heart of innovative thinking, including specific techniques for rechanneling the tensions of conflicting points of view into new ideas and alternative options.

When Sparks Fly explores how all aspects of the work environment, from leadership style to the use of space, sound, even smell, can enhance innovation.

Levitt, Theodore. "Creativity Is Not Enough," *Harvard Business Review* OnPoint Enhanced Edition. Boston: Harvard Business School Publishing, 2002. Creativity is often touted as a miraculous road to organizational growth and affluence. But creative new ideas can hinder rather than help a company if they are put forward irresponsibly. In this article, the author, a professor emeritus at Harvard Business School offers suggestions for the person with a great new idea. First, work with the situation as it is—recognize that the executive is already bombarded with problems. Second, act responsibly by including in your proposal at least a minimal indication of the costs, risks, manpower, and time your idea may involve.

Michalko, Michael. *Cracking Creativity: The Secrets of Creative Genius*. Berkeley, CA: Ten Speed Press, 1998. Michalko divides the topic into two sections—seeing what no one else sees and thinking what no one else is thinking—and provides concrete examples, strategies, and exercises for each. For example, strategies for novel thinking include connecting the unconnected, looking at the other side, and finding what you're not looking for.

Robinson, Alan G., and Sam Stern. *Corporate Creativity*. San Francisco: Berrett-Koehler, 1997. An in-depth analysis of six elements that make for creativity in the work environment: alignment, self-initiated activity, unofficial activity, serendipity, diverse stimuli, and in-company communication.

Skarzynski, Peter, and Rowan Gibson. *Innovation to the Core: A Blueprint for Transforming the Way Your Company Innovates*. Boston: Harvard Business School Press, 2008. Peter Skarzynski and business strategist Rowan Gibson share the accumulated wisdom from Strategos—the consulting firm founded by Gary Hamel and led by Skarzynski that helps clients instill innovation into their very core. Drawing on a wealth of stories and examples, the book shows how companies of every stripe have overcome the barriers to successful, profitable innovation. Readers will find parts devoted to crucial topics, such as how to organize the discovery process, generate strategic insights, enlarge the innovation pipeline, and maximize return on innovation. Frameworks, checklists, and probing questions help put the book's ideas into action.

Sutton, Robert I. *Weird Ideas That Work*. New York: Free Press, 2002. The title says it all. This Stanford professor builds a convincing case for why the standard rules of business management suffocate innovation. In their place he offers unconventional ways to promote and enhance creativity, many of them counterintuitive. He discusses new approaches to hiring, managing creative people, and dealing with risk and randomness in innovation. These practices succeed, he believes, because they increase the range of a company's knowledge, allow people to see old problems in new ways, and help companies break from the past.

Utterback, James M. *Mastering the Dynamics of Innovation.* Boston: Harvard Business School Press, 1994. This work by a noted scholar provides a practical model for business leaders striving to innovate. It anticipated by many years some of the ideas popularized by Clayton Christensen and others. The author draws from historical cases of innovation to illustrate how an innovation enters an industry, how mainstream firms typically respond, and how new and old players wrestle for dominance. He documents the pace of innovation, showing how a wave of process innovation often follows in the footsteps of product innovations that have preceded it. Of special interest is Utterback's notion of the "dominant design," and how such a design gradually evolves from the great variety that often characterizes the early years of ferment associated with the market introduction of new-to-the-world products.

Von Hippel, Eric. *Democratizing Innovation.* Cambridge, MA: MIT Press, 2005. Improvements in computer and communications technology are giving users opportunities to develop or improve their own products and services, and to share what they've learned with others—including product companies. This is a must-read for anyone who wants to better tap the knowledge and insights of customers and potential adopters of new products and services.

_____ . *The Sources of Innovation.* New York: Oxford University Press, 1997. This book presents studies showing that end-users, material suppliers, and others—and not always manufacturers—are the typical sources of innovation in some fields. These findings suggest that R&D people search out lead users as sources of innovative ideas.

Zelinski, Ernie J. *The Joy of Thinking Big.* Berkeley, CA: Ten Speed Press, 1998. This book lacks a cohesive conceptual framework, but its strength lies in the dozens of hands-on tips and strategies for individuals that get at the heart of the creative paradox. Sample topics include how to develop a great memory for forgetting, how to fail successfully, and how to be a creative loafer.

Index

About the Subject Adviser

DR. RALPH KATZ is a professor of entrepreneurship and innovation at Northeastern University's College of Business and is in the Management of Technology Group of M.I.T.'s Sloan School of Management. He has carried out extensive management research on technology-based innovation with emphasis in the management of technical professionals and project teams.

The National Academy of Management awarded Dr. Katz the "New Concept Award" for his contributions to the field of organizational behavior. He is also the recipient of two "Best Paper" awards from *R&D Management*, and the IRI's 2005 Holland Award. The second edition of his book, *The Human Side of Managing Technological Innovation*, was published in 2004.

Dr. Katz received his PhD and MBA from the University of Pennsylvania's Wharton Graduate School and a B.S. in mathematics from Carnegie Mellon University.

About the Writer

RICHARD LUECKE is the writer of several other books in the Harvard Business Essentials series. Based in Salem, Massachusetts, Mr. Luecke has authored or developed more than thirty books and dozens of articles on a wide range of business subjects, including *Scuttle Your Ships Before Advancing* (Oxford University Press, 1994) and *The eBay Phenomenon* (John Wiley & Sons, 2000). He has an MBA from the University of St. Thomas.